Start

A

Black Business

In YOUR Community!

Start now...

Diane Thomas-Newbill

START A
BLACK BUSINESS
IN **YOUR** COMMUNITY

Whether you are age 9 or 90...

Turn your skills into a thriving business!

Start Now...

DIANE THOMAS-NEWBILL

DY-RON DESIGNS

PUBLISHING

Copyright © 2018 by Dy-Ron Designs Publishing. All rights reserved. Printed in the United States of America. Except as permitted under the United States Copyright Act of 1976, no part of this publication may be reproduced or distributed in any form or by any means (electronic, mechanical, photocopy, recording or otherwise) or stored in a database or retrieval system, without the prior written permission of the publisher or the author, except in the case of brief quotations embodied in critical articles and reviews.

Dy-Ron Designs Publishing, Ypsilanti, MI 48198.

Psalm 127.1a- Unless the Lord builds the house, they labor in vain who build it.

ISBN-13: 978-1720517382

ISBN-10: 172051738X

Dy-Ron Designs Publishing books are available on **Amazon.com** in paperback and e-books. After reading this book (paperback or e-book) please take the time to post a review on the Amazon website. Thank you!

For more information, please email us at:

DyRonPublishing@gmail.com or contact your local book store.

Book design and layout by Dy-Ron Designs Publishing.

Editing and Cover design by Dy-Ron Designs Publishing.

Front Cover Image is the sole property of RGBStock.com. All rights are reserved.

Start a Black Business in Your Community/by Diane Thomas-Newbill

**To the person who is so driven to start your own business,
I believe in YOUR success!**

**YOU have to decide in your mind to start here, right now!
Don't let procrastination, fear or the feeling of not being good enough stop you from pushing forward...to create something great!**

If you don't believe that you have the skills or resources to make it happen, keep reading...

My prayer is that this book blesses everyone who reads it. May it give you the courage to go forth and make a difference in YOUR Community and ALL the lives you touch. Amen!

This book is for you!

Diane Thomas-Newbill

Start a Black Business in YOUR Community
Start now....

CONTENTS

Introduction - **6**

Chapter 1: Let's Assess the Neighborhood - **9**

Chapter 2: Zoning in on YOUR Personal Knowledge and Skills - **13**

Chapter 3: Goals and Stereotypes of Black Business - **19**

Chapter 4: Born to Create and Develop (A history to be proud of) - **25**

Chapter 5: Starting Your Business, Let's Begin With YOU - **31**

Chapter 6: Basic Steps to Starting Your Business - **46**

Chapter 7: Go Forward (launch, connect, be an example, make a difference) - **57**

Chapter 8: Our Forefathers of Inventions and Business - **62**

Chapter 9: About the Author - **83**

Chapter 10: Appendix/References - **88**

INTRODUCTION

Welcome to Start a Black Business in Your Community! This is not a book to read and then put upon a shelf. In order for you to reach your desired goal and destination...it is imperative that you **"decide"** to follow through and **immediately work everyday** to build your black business in your community.

Why should you start YOUR black business now? Read the following information taken from the 2012 U.S. Census Bureau, <u>and then you</u> **decide**:

THE POWER OF BUSINESS OWNERSHIP

White-owned businesses: Create 55.9 million jobs which is enough to employ **44%** of the working-age White population, and with annual revenues of $12.9 Trillion they could give **EVERY** working-age White American a check for <u>$102,000</u> **EVERY YEAR.**

Asian-owned businesses: Create 3.8 million jobs which is enough to employ **33%** of the working-age Asian population, and with annual revenues of $793.5 Billion they could give **EVERY** working-age Asian American a check for <u>$67,000</u> **EVERY YEAR.**

Hispanic-owned businesses: Create 2.5 million jobs which is enough to employ **8%** of the working-age Hispanic population, and with annual revenues of $473.6 Billion they could give **EVERY** working-age Hispanic American a check for $14,000 **EVERY YEAR.**

Black-owned businesses: Create 1 million jobs which is enough to employ **4%** of the working-age Black population, and with annual revenues of $187.6 Billion they could give **EVERY** working-age Black American a check for $7,000 **EVERY YEAR.**

I say "Come on! YOU owe it to YOUR family and community!" **Start now...**

Information concerning the above demographics: jobs = hired employees. This does not include owners of businesses who only employ themselves. Source: U.S. Census Bureau 2012 Survey of Business Owners, 2012 Census Bureau Annual Estimates of the Resident Population by Sex, Single Year of Age, Race, and Hispanic Origin for the United States Population Division Black-owned business: Blacks or African Americans own 51 percent or more of the equity, interest, or stock of the business. Working-age adults ages 18-64. All figures rounded. This information is also accredited to: BlackDemographics.com

How is this book different than the average **start something** book, you might ask? Read on:

Objective: The goal is to inspire you to get off the couch, **"decide"** on the skills that WILL help you create wealth (better income and lifestyle) for yourself, family and community through building YOUR own business.

This book is not a get rich quick scheme. It will not make you rich over night, but will inspire you to start making money as soon as possible. Basically, if you use your own determination, knowledge, skills and do research in the areas that interest you...you can't fail! Of course, persistence is the key. If you will dedicate just an hour a day (at first) to building it...it will grow.

This book is not a book to put down any societies or groups defined by demographic criteria such as nationality, religion, ethnicity, sex or education.

It is intended to educate you on the demographics of business ownership, and "hopefully" give you the boost to help change the BLACK BUSINESS empowerment. Yes, I said empowerment! Money does change the lifestyle, which includes home ownership, investments, and yes, the environment YOU live in. Of course, the objective is to create the business **in** your neighborhood. This is very important. As you continue reading this book, you will understand why creating the business inside your own community is so important.

By the way, this book is not a step by step, start a business book. I will give you an outline of the steps to take to build one, but not forms, etc. I will share my knowledge and research, hoping to bring you closer to YOUR Black Enterprise.

Shall we begin?
Okay, let's **start now...**

Chapter 1

Let's Assess the Neighborhood

Let's begin at the very beginning of why you should start **YOUR** Black Business in **YOUR** own neighborhood...

If we walk or drive through your neighborhood, I can bet that the party stores (or local stores), hair and beauty supply stores, gas stations, banks, restaurants, etc., are pretty much owned by someone other than a Black Business. I also can bet that these establishments have a scarce few (if any) of black employees. To go even deeper, I can also bet that even though the establishment is in YOUR neighborhood...many times you feel like you are being watched or not trusted as you shop in these stores. If you are treated fairly, I applaud those establishments.

To go a little further into what I am trying to explain here, more than likely the owners of these establishments live in another town/city...or what we call a "better, upscale" neighborhood. Yes, they sell their products to you, work their own employees (mostly their family or ethnic group), and take the money back to their own neighborhoods.

I hope this information makes you think about the importance of establishing our own, in our own neighborhoods. There is nothing wrong with "anyone" establishing a business. I am not knocking the other ethnic groups who are determined enough to build wealth and a future for their own.

I often wonder if we tried to establish these same types of businesses in their neighborhoods, such as: hair and beauty, gas stations, cell phone outlets, restaurants, local party stores, etc., if they would welcome us, or even buy from us. This is not a discriminating statement, but a reality check.

My personal assessment of some of the conditions in the neighborhoods:

Our black neighborhoods have been labeled as slums, poor, unattractive, among other things. Some of the fault is ours, I do admit…but some of the problem is the businesses that come into our neighborhoods. I am talking about the businesses that set up, and pretend to be doing "the people of the neighborhood" a favor. Some of the businesses that offer these favors are local party stores, grocery stores and gas stations. Read on:

Heard of a "Ghost town"? They look like closed, run down businesses that give the neighborhood the look of desertion.

Here are some of the favors offered:

If you own a bridge card, they will do you a favor by letting you "buy" whatever you need that is not food…because they are helping you! The only problem is that if your bridge card is scanned, sooner or later you will be part of an investigation. Once the party store, gas station or whatever has the reputation of making these deals, eventually the information will get back to the law. You risk the chance of losing your benefits, and may pay hefty fines. The store gets raided and eventually is shut down! Now we have started the "Ghost town" process. In some cities right now, you will see many party stores and gas stations closed, some even boarded up or with high weeds around them. Eventually, you will even see trash/debris on the landscape.
But remember, the store was only trying to help you! Hmm…
Their goal is to make as much money as they can, regardless of what it is costing you!

Here is another example: Have you ever heard of local stores and gas stations selling a "Lucy"?

If you can't afford a pack of cigarettes that may cost you $8 for a pack of 20, they will sell you how ever many you need out of a pack...which they call a LUCY. You can by 2 for $2. How about 8 for $8? This is a win for them, because at that rate, you will be spending $20 for 20 cigarettes, instead of $8 for a pack. Of course, they are only thinking of you, right? Truthfully, they want all of your money! If you can't afford $8, they will take your pennies, dimes, nickels, etc. Just bring in the money!

How about the grocery stores that try to bring in cheaper prices by selling you spoiled meat? Yes, the grocery store that starts up, and within months leave because of their poor quality of meat and product. And guess what? When they leave...they add to the "Ghost town". Of course, it always looks like **we** are destroying the neighborhoods, but in reality these people don't live in the neighborhood, so they don't really care of the conditions. **Somewhere, we have to start to care enough...to make the change in our own neighborhoods!**

One of the strangest things to me is the hair care and beauty supply stores in the neighborhoods. If you are a "black woman" and you walk into a beauty supply store, you more than likely see someone of the Asian descent running the store. If you have black owners in your hair care and beauty supply store...I applaud them!!! We all know that black hair is of a different texture. Being a black woman myself, I am actually pretty proud of my so called "wooly" hair. To make a point though, if you being black... need hair grease, hair weave, or shampoo...does the Asian person really know what the best product is for you? Probably not! Well to be honest...NO! They really have no clue, since they don't use it in their own hair. Here is where a "Black" owner really is needed. Also, as you stroll throughout the beauty supply store, how many black employees are actually working there? So, even though the owner might be Asian, wouldn't they think you could identify with a black employee telling you about the product? **By the way, when I say an employee, I mean a real employee...on a time clock!**

So, I conclude my assessment by saying... "Right now, **decide** to change the 'Ghost town', and the ownership of the establishments in YOUR neighborhood." Use your skills and the knowledge of what you have acquired through education and life experience. If you cut grass, cut it with pride. If you do hair, do it with style. If you are good with money, run a store or a bank. Start somewhere. If you babysit, start a daycare. If you love teaching, start a tutoring business. Love flowers? Start a nursery...or even plant flowers for a living as a landscaping expert. I can go on and on. You have the skills...I know you do!   Don't stop now...keep reading! I am so ready for you to be ready to START NOW...on YOUR black business endeavor.

Chapter 2

Zoning in on YOUR Personal Knowledge and Skills

Let's zone right in on your talents. Your knowledge is the use of your mind, and your skills are your crafty unique gifts, whether tech, singing, washing walls, etc.

Everyone has many talents just waiting to come out! Let's tap into yours...

Understand that every morning you are born again to do something great. You just have to "**decide**" to do it! You probably have never heard this phrase before, but you have to find "your definite purpose". The **definite purpose** is the thing that you are willing to eat, drink, and sleep over. None of your time will feel wasted when you are working on your definite purpose.

We will focus more on discovering what YOUR definite purpose is later in this chapter. For now, know that once you know what your definite purpose is, you will have to be active every day (at least 5 days) to become closer to bringing it into fruition. Even when obstacles show up, and they will...you will have to "**decide**" to move like the clock, FORWARD. Time is important!

Have you noticed that I use the word "**decide**" quite often? It is because your success depends on you! Life (including business) is definitely about the sowing and the reaping.

Read the following passages from the bible:

2 Corinthians 9:6 : *But this I say, He which soweth sparingly shall reap also sparingly; and he which soweth bountifully shall reap also bountifully.*

Galatians 6:7 : *Be not deceived; God is not mocked, for whatever a man soweth, that shall he also reap.*

A key point to keep in mind is that Nature gives ABUNDANCE. An example is planting a seed. If you plant an apple seed, the tree will yield more than one apple.

So here and now, determine where you are going. Free your mind of fear and doubt. Let your thoughts be about success. Have a can do mentality. BELIEVE that you can accomplish all that you set out to do. Truthfully, if you "decide" to do it…you can't fail.

One of my personal mottos for myself is: **Keep going.** I let these words play in my mind, especially during those times when I feel like giving up or procrastinating. In the long run, the things I "decide" to do, I seem to always accomplish them.

I hope that I have given you the motivation to want to move forward now. Let's look at the options all around you. As stated before, it doesn't matter if you are age 9 or 90. If you are 9 years old, you could do something as simple as pulling weeds from the local neighbor's flowerbeds. There are numerous things that you can do. I often use this example: If my granddaughter needed to make $20; she could take $10 to a dollar store. She could buy 10 items and have a little yard sale (selling each item for $2). Just that quick, she has made $20! To make even more money, she could go to the grocery store and buy a 12 can generic box of lemonade. Hopefully, the day is a warm one…in which, she could sell single cans of lemonade during her yard sale for $1. Here's the math: the box of can lemonade will have 12 to a box. The price will range no higher than $5 to purchase from the grocery store.

From that one box she will make $12, which will be a $7 profit. So, all together she has spent no more than $15 ($10 at dollar store and $5 for lemonade), but she has yielded a total of $32, and a profit of $17.

From my example, you can see there are numerous ways even for a 9 year old to make some money. **Enterprise should be shown to our youth as soon as they can understand it!**
If you are old enough to babysit, get started if you have the patience for children. The same is true for cutting grass, etc. I suggest these things to our youth, because so many have become "couch potatoes". The market is now very easy to step into! Right now, you could have the whole neighborhood as your clients for lawn care, pulling weeds, dog walking, etc. Get started now…

For the adults…starting your business will be a lot different. First you will have to decide what you want to bring to the market. Once you have decided your product or service, you will have to take out an assumed name, and if you decide to have employees, register for an employer identification number (federal), and also register for your local state taxes. We will discuss this more thoroughly in Chapter 6 (Basic Steps to Starting YOUR Business).

Let's explore some products or services that <u>**you**</u> can start up in YOUR neighborhood. Of course, the list could go on for days; therefore, I will suggest only a few. Keep in mind that this is just a list of case scenarios, but you will have to do the homework yourself to determine what is good for you.

First of all, I would suggest that if you have been in a field for awhile (meaning as a career), tapping into that skill as an enterprise could be beneficial. Let's say you have been working as a maintenance technician for a local apartment complex, those skills could be used to start your own "handyman" service, or you could single out just one service. For instance, you could offer a painting service or a general maintenance service.

Another case, let's say you have worked as an office assistant, in which you have learned many computer programs. You've also learned typing at a pretty good speed. Starting a typing firm for legal documents is one suggestion. You could do research online on how to fill out the documents, download blank copies of the documents, and go from there.

I use legal as an *idea,* but there are so many types of businesses that need documents typed.

Not only can you type documents, you can tap into other types of services needed from your experience in computer programs. Again, do some research and from that, create a list of the services you want to offer in your new enterprise.

How about a daycare or a hairdresser? If you can braid, curl, wash, and or perm hair...start there. The businesses that I'm suggesting here can be started as a home-based business. If you are tech savvy, how about starting a web design business that helps set up blogs? The list could go on.

If you have the patience to go outside of the home-based realm, you could start a non-profit or for-profit business using funding or grants. The SBA (Small Business Association) and organizations like SCORE can give you help in obtaining more information and resources. There are other groups as well, but this is a start. I suggest these, because many of the other organizations require you to join with a hefty fee.

Bottom line, whatever your craft...get started. If you fix things or tinker with things, make that a business. Some things you may need to obtain a license to become legal (e.g. auto mechanic). Please keep in mind that this is a list, but you have to "research" if you will need a license for your area of expertise.

If you are retiring from a field, and you have the resources (saved money) to start a business...think about a local party store, a hair care facility, gas station or bank. They are desperately needed in the black neighborhoods. If your business can't be right in the neighborhood, try to get your business as close to it as you can. After establishing it, market to the neighborhoods...especially offering jobs to our black youth. Yes, please give them a chance. Remember that you were once a black youth, and that "someone" gave you a chance. I can't stress how much we need to educate our youth on black enterprise.

Here's another suggestion: If you are good at sewing or even knitting, start a service that makes clothes for animals (cats and dogs). People are very close to their pets these days. The pets are now extended family. This service will definitely yield a hefty sum! Also, if you sew, think about creating "preemie clothing" for babies born underweight. You could market to hospitals in their newborn departments.

If you are crafty, create a special product. It could be dogs, dolls, rugs, furniture, etc. you created. If you are tech savvy, make your craft do something physical. Just like that, you have a product! Just try something. Keep trying until you are so satisfied with it. The Key...**Do Not Give Up!**

As said before, there are so many businesses you could start right in your neighborhood. How about a local arcade? Gaming is such a big deal these days. How many gaming arcades are in your neighborhood? Do your research, and get busy! **Decide** and start now...

Your Definite Purpose:

From here we will discover your definite purpose. You have to decide what you want to do, and then, you have to put it in stone. Yes, write down what you want to do, what you want to yield from it (in numeral figures) and start. From what you wrote down, create a small plan. If you are trying to make $10 or $10,000, put it in writing. Set a date of when you want it completely accomplished. Create a "Statement of Purpose". Here's an example:

I want to start a daycare that will yield $40,000 by 12/31/20--. I plan to register my assumed name by: 1/20/20--. I will check into any required legal procedures by: 2/20/20--. Through this service I will provide excellent quality and quantity of service. I believe in this so deeply that I can see it already.

The above statement of purpose is just an example so that you can see what you have to do. Please tailor it to your desired area. It is imperative that you know your "definite" plan. There is no maybe, it has to be definite. No procrastination. No one day a week. No only when I feel like it attitude. It is a definite thing! You can't fail...and you can't quit!!! Like my motto says: Keep going! **Start now...**

*A note about youth businesses: As mentioned above, there are many services that can be started. Taking out an assumed name for a youth business and the filing of other business papers should be done and overseen by the parents/adults who care for the youth. Therefore, when I talk about the adults starting a business (in chapter 6), it also covers the youth services...if the adults are willing to run it legally as a business (assuming total responsibility), becoming the manager for their child's service.

Chapter 3

Goals and Stereotypes of Black Business

We all know that not every black male will be a professional basketball player or a rapper. Not every black female is outspoken, nor is she at home with one or two babies waiting on a handout. Yet society often looks at black people through these types of lenses.

Black business also has a very biased perception that is very similar to the scenarios above. In this chapter we will discuss the goals and stereotypes associated to the black business sector.

Let's start with GOALS:

Despite what you may hear around your neighborhood, there are organizations out there that are fighting for the "black business". One group that is setting goals for "you" are the United States Black Chambers, Inc (USblackchamber.org)

Here are their goals for African-American Businesses:

They are spearheading what they call "Black Wealth 2020". It is an initiative to close the financial gap between White and Black families by 2020. They have partnered with over 22 other organizations to help build Black wealth.

The goal is to increase the number of Black home ownership by 2 million, increase the number of Black Businesses to 4 million, to increase Black annualized revenue, and to increase the number of African-Americans banking at Black banks.

They have developed an application for Android and iPhone users, to help them find Black businesses in their own neighborhoods.

According to the United States Black Chamber, there are over 101,000 Black businesses in the application's directory.

Please take the time to visit their website (USBlackChamber.org) for more information about what they are currently doing.

Of course, there are other organizations out there that support black business, but I wanted to share at least one. How encouraging it is to see leaders out their carrying the torch! We need to grab it, and be willing to pass it on to the next generation. If we don't, what kind of future are we offering to the generations to come?

On a personal level, it is imperative that "you" set goals as to why you are starting your business, and what you plan to achieve. Don't make very small goals, but obtainable and realistic ones. If you BELIEVE it, you truly can achieve it. As mentioned before, research that idea!

A note here: there will always be people who will tell you that your idea sounds stupid...that you can't obtain the goals you have set. Only YOU can make it a reality, but you have to **"decide"** to do it! **Start now...**

I won't tell you what goals to set, but I will say that they should at least entail the following:

- Type of service or product you are bringing to the market
- The amount of sales you plan to make the first year
- Who you plan to market to (e.g. jump rope...for girls, gyms, etc.)
- How many of your widgets (service/product) you have to sell to reach your financial goal
- How much you plan to personally make as a owner's wage

- If your product or service is more about helping the community, state...what you plan to achieve in the community
- VERY IMPORTANT: <u>dates</u> to achieve these goals (e.g. $100,000 in sales by: 12/31/20--).

If you are a family business, I would suggest that you set family financial goals as well. If you are helping a child start a business, sit down with your little person and set goals! Again, it is so important to teach our youth about money and good spending habits.

I would also like to add here the importance of setting the example for our youth. They need to see us finding joy and accomplishment into what we are doing. Who wants to do something that always looks like it is dreaded? No matter what business you decide to do, take **PRIDE** in knowing that "**YOU**" are making it happen.

I cannot stress enough the importance of "knowing" your product or service so well that you can recite it easily if someone asks about it. You have to be the expert in your field, if you expect someone to listen. You <u>must</u> give a good product or service. It is a <u>must</u>, because repeat customers are **the key** to you reaching your financial goals. You <u>must</u> have loyal customers who believe in your service or product. Not only will your loyal customers keep buying, but they will spread the word to others (Word of mouth). Yes, word of mouth is definitely the best way to get customers. Let each product or service you give be <u>excellent!</u> I implore you to pay special attention to the sentences above that stress **must**. If you don't get this part right, you will not keep customers or reach your financial goals.

Now let's look at many of the stereotypes that are associated with "Black Business". I must say, because of the stereotypes...it makes it harder for a black business that is really working hard to create something great. So to all the black businesses **not** setting a good example...<u>shame on you!</u>

Before we go into the stereotypes, I must say that creating Black wealth has nothing to do with selling drugs or anything illegal. If you are doing this right now, "decide" today to stop and create something beneficial for your neighborhood, youth, family and generations to come.

Make a product or service that you can brag about and have a logo, title and reputable clients for. Make a product or service that will last for generations. If you wonder why I keep stressing that you are to do it for the generations to come, read the following bible passage:

Proverbs 13:22 –A good man leaveth an inheritance to his children's children

Yes, even the bible let's us know that it is our duty to look out for the generations that follow!

Let's look into the Stereotypes that have given us bad reputations:

Even though it is true that Black businesses have seen growth over the years, they still have the stigma of being less organized, having inferior products or services, and the reputation of having less when it comes to resources.

It's sad to say, but the majority of our black people will buy from the White, Asian and Hispanic before they will buy from a Black business. Of course, this means that the money spent is still going into other neighborhoods and enriching businesses that are not Black Business. Again, I say that it is not a racial thing, but a "building and empowerment" thing. We have got to "decide" to support black business by buying from them. **Even if this book doesn't inspire you to start your own black business, I hope it will encourage you to start buying more from black businesses in your area.**

While there are a lot of black businesses that don't have the resources to run big businesses, keep in mind that the other groups (White, Asian, Hispanic, etc.) have quite a few small businesses too. There are resources for minorities to help get your business started (just like for the Asian and Hispanic). If you can get the help, get it! If you don't need it, then go forth without it. Either way, don't let someone make you feel that you can't start something because of the financial resources. Start with what you have and build. Even if you start out small, at least you have started. Also, if you would get involved in your neighborhood with other businesses (whether black or white businesses), you will find opportunities that you never knew existed. I also ask that if you are successful in starting your business, that as you develop your business, please help another black business to get started (even if it is only mentoring).

The bottom line is that with all the negative stereotypes associated with the black business, you can make your business stand out. Be strong on giving excellent quality and quantity. Let your product or service have a reputation of being the best out there. Treat each customer with respect. As long as the cash is green, it doesn't matter who spent it. If you can collaborate with other businesses (even if they aren't black), it is a plus. I must stress that I'm not saying not to do business with businesses that aren't black. I am saying to support black business. Help us to create Black Wealth for the generations to come.

Let our youth feel good in the neighborhoods and feel that they can have nice things in an honest way. **We are hard working people. We are intelligent people, but we have to start BELIEVING it ourselves.**

I am often tickled when I hear people say that the slaves were illiterate. If you send me to China right now, I definitely couldn't read their books. It doesn't make me illiterate, but unable to understand another language.

Therefore, even though many of the slaves couldn't read, they sure were able to create inventions that have carried America a long way! Black people, you are intelligent, you are gifted. Use your gifts! **Start now...**

Chapter 4

Born to Create and Develop (A history to be proud of)

If you look around your settings right now, you will discover that every item you see was once a thought (an idea). Yes, the television, cell phone, even the couch and chair you sit on. We all are gifted with a great wealth of intelligence, yet most don't understand or utilize it. We often think that only a small number of people can be genius.

In this chapter we will discuss how you were born to create wonderful things. To understand this "truth" fully, you have to develop the mindset that will lead you to your genius.

I hope that you won't feel offended by my next comment, but "Laziness and being comfortable where we are, keeps us from reaching our full potential". Let me share an example of how the mind (your thoughts) can change your circumstances. Read the example below:

Karen was often depressed. I don't know if she was depressed because she ate too much, consumed too much alcohol, or because she never took the time to exercise. Either way, she was always depressed, so she would lie around feeling sorry for herself and her circumstances.

When she finally went to the doctor, because her health had become so bad...she was diagnosed with cancer. She came home still depressed, but began to read the pamphlets given to her. She began watching motivational cancer success videos on Youtube, and she joined a social support group. During her "cancer" journey...she discovered that she wanted to live!

*At that period in her life, she **"decided"** to do everything that she could to change her chances for survival. From that moment on, without joining an alcohol support group, she stopped drinking. Without joining an support group for overeating, she began to make better eating habits, and without all the fads of diet pills and numerous exercise machines, she starting on the path of walking everyday.*

*You see, until Karen "decided" to develop her mind to create a better life for herself, she wasn't living life full of potential. She was just getting by, slowly destroying her health and life. She was actually LAZY and COMFORTABLE where she was in life. Now Karen has defeated the cancer, and has developed a healthy attitude which makes her excited to "live" each day to its full potential. She has "decided" to be happy in life. Yes, her attitude...or positive thoughts changed her circumstances. She could have just accepted the cancer and waited her time out, still overeating and indulging in alcohol (feeling sorry for herself), but she **"decided"** to get up and do something to change her situation.*

I used the story of Karen as an example of how our minds (thoughts) create our circumstances.

So let us go on a journey to help develop your mind into discovering your genius (creativity).

Another example of the mindset changing the situation is during the time of African-Americans in slavery. During this period, even though they were considered illiterate in the eyes of the white man, African-Americans used their minds (intelligence) and skills (crafty ways) to create inventions to actually make their jobs easier. Inventions that we now take for granted (e.g. the baby carriage).

Before I go any further, I must remind you of the Higher Power that gives us the wisdom, strength and knowledge to do something great. Yes, even our forefathers knew of the intervention of the Higher Power. Seek God in ALL your endeavors. Each day pray for His wisdom and guidance. He truly does bless His people and His creation. Read the following bible passage about putting God in all we do:

Psalm 127.1a – *Unless the Lord builds the house, they labor in vain who build it.*

I personally live by the above scripture and I use it as a signature at the bottom of all my business emails that go out. I also have it as our company motivational scripture.

In this chapter I would like to share a few inventions created/developed by Black people. For a more detailed description of inventions and Businesses created by Black people… see Chapter 8: Our Forefathers of Inventions and Business.

Let's start with **Garrett Morgan**. *He invented the traffic light and the gas mask. Garrett was born in Kentucky in 1877. It is said that he created the traffic light after noticing so many accidents on busy intersections. He also created the gas mask which was used to help the workers after an underground explosion.*

Have you ever heard of **Lewis Latimer**? *He was born in 1848 to runaway slaves. Lewis became an inventor and engineer. He invented one of the earliest air conditioning units. He also helped in the development of some of the world's greatest inventions which included the light bulb and the telephone.*

*Here's another: **Thomas Elkins**. Yes, Thomas created the modern toilet! In 1872 he created the "Chamber Commode", which included a mirror, and washstand.*

*How about **Benjamin Banneker** who was born to freed slaves in 1731? He was truly a gifted creator. Benjamin was an astronomer, author, inventor, surveyor, and mathematician. He invented clocks and published six almanacs which included political and social commentary. In each almanac he advocated for the rights of slaves and free blacks.*

*Let's talk about the blood bank. Who invented the modern blood banks? **Charles Drew** invented the blood banks! He was born in Washington in 1904. He was a surgeon, researcher and inventor. Can you believe that since World War II...his invention has saved so many lives?*

*Even though I have been mentioning Black inventors in America, let's travel to Nigeria, Africa. Yes, I'm talking about **Philip Emeagwali**. He was born in Nigeria in 1954. Do you know that Philip created the world's fastest computer in 1989? Seldom do we hear about people like him, but he earned many advanced degrees including a PH.D in scientific computing!*

*Here's another hero that definitely helped during war times...**Frederick Jones**. Frederick was a self-taught engineer. Even though he created other inventions, he was known most for his refrigeration machine used to transport blood, food and medicine during World War II.*

*I'm so excited about all the inventions black people have made. My heart is skipping a beat! Therefore, I will tell you about **Daniel Hale Williams**. Daniel was born in Pennsylvania in 1856. He became a physician and a surgeon. Would you believe that in 1891 he founded the first integrated hospital? Wow...impressive!*

Two years later, he became the first person to successfully complete open heart surgery.

Just mentioning these few Black people should make you realize that "**You**" were definitely born to create and/or develop something great! Keep reading...

Did I tell you about "The Wealthiest Colored Man in the Northwest"? Yes, **Alexander Miles** was known as the wealthiest colored man in the northwest. He actually improved the elevator. Alexander created an automatic device to open and close elevator doors. Every time you get in an elevator now...think of Alexander, the Black man who made it a luxury!

Even though I have mentioned all males so far in this chapter, let me mention at least one great female. Of course, Chapter 8 will mention more woman as well as men. For now, let's talk about **Patricia Bath**. Patricia is an inventor and ophthalmologist from Harlem, New York. She is the first black female doctor to receive a medical patent. In 1986 she invented the Laserphaco Probe. The Laserphaco Probe was designed for the treatment of cataracts. Well done, Patricia!

*The information given above about the black inventions was taken from The Congressional Black Caucus Foundation/The Village. The article was posted on February 27, 2015 by Lindsay Gary.

Just like the Black people mentioned above, YOU have the creativity inside of you. So you may never be a doctor or a scientist, but whatever you decide to do...leave your mark! When you read Chapter 8, you will be surprised and proud to know that Black people have made such an impact in our world. The sad part is that most black people don't even know how much we have brought to this world.

If nothing else, I hope this book will enlighten you on the importance "we" bring to not only a continent, but to the world!

I don't know if the children of today use their minds like we did back in the day. With technology such as gaming systems and bingeing on cable and Internet series, there is little time to free the mind for invention. Here is an example: My brother loved basketball so much that he would ball up pieces of paper and toss them at a trash can. Eventually, he took a crate and cut the bottom out, to make a basketball hoop in the back yard. Yes, he nailed it to the tree. Of course, all the guys in the neighborhood eventually made it "the spot". Not being able to buy a basketball hoop didn't stop my brother from making his own.

Another example is the barbecue pit. Those old fashioned ones, made from bricks, made from barrels, you name it...we made it. The barbecue was the best! My greatest memory of a barbecue pit was one made by my ex-husband when our children were small. He was totally genius! The pit was actually a picnic table at one end, but it had a slot carved into it. Inside the slot was a large barbecue barrel that he had made. You could sit at the picnic table and watch the food cooking. All our neighbors were envious! We always said we would market it, but we never did.

Of course, these are small examples of creativity, but I want you to see that if you have a desire for something...make it! There is an invention, a business, something great inside of you! Please..."**decide**" and **Start now!**

Chapter 5

Starting Your Business, Let's Begin With YOU

In the previous chapters, so far we have talked about the importance of starting a business in your own neighborhood, and the impact other businesses have in your community. We have discussed that YOU have the skills and knowledge to succeed at whatever you put your mind and hands to, provided that you "**decide**" and believe that you can accomplish it. Remember that deciding means even through the hard times, you won't give up, you won't quit!

We've also talked about the negative stereotypes associated with Black business and Black people in general. Throughout the previous chapters we have discussed the importance of building something great for the generations to come. In the last chapter, we even talked about the inventions that Black people have created that have made a great difference in the lives we live today. Yes, they have created something that they are passing to the generations that follow. We have to grab the torch and run with it!

When we talked about zoning in on your personal knowledge and skills in chapter two, we briefly talked about you finding your "definite purpose". As mentioned previously, your definite purpose is <u>that something</u> you will lose sleep over. You will be so driven for it to succeed that you will give up your everyday pleasures to accomplish it. In this chapter, I want to dig deeper into helping you understand and develop YOUR definite purpose.

This chapter is designed to help you develop a "mental attitude" to go forth with your Black business. In the next chapter (Chapter 6), I will share the basic steps to starting your business. Before we move into that direction though, you have to understand what you want to build, invent, create... Please don't just read this chapter, but keep an open mind and think deeply as you read this chapter. **The goal of this chapter is to spark something <u>great</u> inside of you!**

Let's begin...

So far, I have mentioned things that you can do around your neighborhood that even a 9 year old can do. I mention these things because it is important for our youth to understand how to make honest money, and to develop good spending habits. Of course, I know as an adult you have skills and knowledge that stem from education and work experience. More than likely you have worked somewhere that has given you skills as an expert. Even a teenager has developed skills from working a fast food job, which they seldom realize. Here is an example: If they have worked the phones or taken the orders...they have developed customer service skills. If they have run a cash register, they have learned money skills. If they have had to put away supplies, they have learned about inventory. Surely, they have had to tidy up the place when business is slow; therefore, they know the importance of keeping the standard of cleaning up in the work place.

Hmm...sounds like a lot of skills in running a business. You see, in business you have to have great customer service. Someone has to take the orders and relate to the customer. You have to know how to serve your customers so well that they feel special with every encounter. In business you have to know inventory or understand the supplies you need. You also need to keep your quality up, including your appearance and work environment. Of course, you definitely have to know how to handle the "money" part of the business...this is a must!

Seldom does the teenager realize that he has learned so many business skills working in fast food. I need to mention that when I use fast food as an example for teenagers, I am not putting down the adults who work in fast food. *There is great potential in fast food. Purchasing a franchise is always a plus in the neighborhood. We definitely need to develop these types of businesses for ourselves as Black people, whether starting the business as a start-up or as a franchise.*

Mentally I want you to understand that there is no bad business, unless it is an illegal business. Anything that goes against the law or harms someone else is considered "bad business". I will add though that the characteristics of the leaders (ethics and personality) can harm a business. In these cases, unless the leader changes his/her attitude or is removed... the business will fail. I also might add that no matter what business you are in (fast food, cutting grass, cleaning, construction, tech, etc.) YOU are a business! Don't feel inferior or look down on anyone who is trying to use their entrepreneurial skills. *It takes great courage, determination and hard work to run a business.* I applaud all who are willing to not only talk about it, but are actually "doing it"!

Finding your definite purpose might be fairly easy for some, and quite difficult for others. Most people have a dream of something they have always wanted to do, but never had the courage to see it through. It may be nothing that you did as a career, but a talent that has been stored up inside of you. There are many people who may have worked in an office all their lives, but actually love working with wood, plants, animals, food, etc.

I knew an elderly man who lived in the neighborhood who had retired from his job. He had the nickname Birdman, because he made wooden bird houses that people traveled miles to buy. His bird houses where unique in design. You could tell that he put a lot of love into them.

When I was a little girl, I remember a man in the neighborhood who made flower pots out of old car tires. When the tires were cut, the flower pot stood up and looked like a flower in design. These are two examples of people using their minds and hands to create something people want.

I must add that you need to create, build, or invent something that is a "want or need". Just like the inventors I talked about previously, they created something that there was a need for. As you decide on what your creation will be, think of how it will impact lives and the communities around you. It may even impact the whole world!

If you worked at a school and loved teaching children (whether teacher, paraprofessional or coach), start something in your neighborhood that could impact the children's lives. If you are a coach or have a love for sports, start a community recreation center that offers sports like basketball, baseball, soccer, etc. If this is too big to start at once, start small. You could offer to coach a team or teams at a local park. Another idea is renting out space at a local school or center in the evenings or on weekends.

As I write this, I am reminded of when I was a little girl... our elementary school held movie day on Saturdays. You could actually go watch movies Saturday mornings. I don't know if the school actually sponsored it themselves, or if someone rented it out for the youth to see movies. The point is that it was local, the kids were familiar with the school setting and it kept the youth active and out of trouble.

Of course, science has advanced so much since my youth days. With all the technical gadgets of today, if you have skills in technology, develop a product! If you can create coding for electronics, do that. If you need to develop more skills for whatever you want to do, learn the skills.

There are so many ways now to advance your knowledge. The Internet has made it possible. Whatever you are interested in... Google it... or search for it on Youtube. Truthfully, **there is no excuse not to do what you are interested in doing**. If you need to go back to school for a certification or license...do it! To be honest, if you choose to do nothing, that is a choice you decided to make.

With the hairstyles that Black people love, there is always a need for that type of business. Our handsome black men love the special hair cuts, and our lovely black women love the crafty designs that truly make us unique. Whether it is braiding, weave or using our own hair, we know how to wear it wonderfully. So, start a hair salon or a barber shop in the neighborhood. If you want to sell the hair products instead, start a beauty supply store.

Have you always loved cars, and painted model cars as a child? Did you work in a car body shop? Have you dealt with paints throughout your life? Take the time to research, to see what you need to do to start a body shop in your neighborhood. If you need a certification or license...or more skills, get them.

If you are currently still working a job, you should start now in developing the skills needed to venture out into your entrepreneurial business. Start your research now. Explore your options and begin to put it all together. Remember the current job is the option right now, but it is not where you intend to be later in life. I implore you to at least work part-time in your venture, even if you are currently working a job. It will take a little sacrifice, but it will definitely pay off!

You don't have to actually invent a new product. If you have an idea on how to improve a current product, research...research...research, and then come up with a solution.

Do you remember the days when your school had the science fairs? You would have to come up with a problem to solve (invention, etc), do some research on the subject and form a hypothesis. You would have to explain your solution to the problem on the display board. If you were very clever at your science project you might come in first, second or third place. You actually won a ribbon! Well, in this situation you might not win a ribbon, but you will help a cause in developing a product or service, give opportunity to people looking for a job, and take pride in knowing that you followed up on your dream. **Keep in mind that you set the standard of your business and determine how much you want to make financially every year.** Yes, the money potential is up to you. You will have to **"decide"** and do it! As I have previously repeated in every chapter, you will also be adding another Black business to your community and building for the generations to come. **Start now…**

I believe you now understand that it is up to YOU to **"decide"** on your definite purpose. Hopefully, I have sparked something in you that have given you ideas. If you need to get in a quiet spot and reflect on what you want to bring to the market, take the time and do so.

Once you have **"decided"** on your definite purpose, YOU have to believe that it can be accomplished. In the rest of this chapter, we will focus on developing your mental attitude. Yes, you have to have a positive mental attitude if you want to succeed. There are going to be obstacles in front of you. You may even encounter friends, relatives, or what have you, that will try to discourage you. If you let those things defeat you, you will give up. You have to **"decide"** right now, no matter what the circumstances…that you won't quit…you won't give up!

Put inside you mind that you don't want to just start, but that you want to be a finisher. Whatever the product or service is that you will be bringing to the market place; you have to know it so deeply.

You really have to become an expert in your field. You also have to demand that your product or service will always deliver top quality, and that you will have excellent quantity. Let me explain: the top quality means every product or service you deliver will ALWAYS be the best. No skimping on service. The excellent quantity means that you will deliver the best service each time, which will make repeat customers. **The key to growing the business is the repeat customers;** therefore, **you want to sell 100 widgets to a customer instead of only 1.** Of course, this means that they have to believe in your service or product.

It is beneficial to display positive affirmations around you to keep you encouraged. I have displayed next to my computer the words "keep going". It really helps on a day that I might feel discouraged, or lazy. We all have something inside of us that makes us doubt or procrastinate...so don't feel that you are the only one. If you have one of those days, and you slack, don't stop. Get up the next day and be better!

I have stressed the **"decide"** factor quite often in this book to you. You see, when you decide on something, you have put it into your subconscious mind. Your subconscious mind works continuously. The more you begin to think on accomplishing the task of starting your Black Business; you will develop the mindset of wanting to see it come to fruition. The subconscious mind has more impact on what you do...more than you could even imagine.

Consider the following bible verse:

Proverbs 23:7: As a man thinketh in his heart, so is he.

This bible verse is really an important verse to consider. It clearly tells us whether positive or negative, what we think in our heart is what it will be. Therefore, the more you think of your losses, you attract more losses. This also lets us see that if we think more in a positive way, we will attract more positive outcomes.

There is a difference with the subconscious mind and the conscious mind. The subconscious mind can't determine the good from the bad. Whatever you put into the subconscious mind, it works to accomplish. Therefore, if you are thinking negatively in the subconscious mind, change your thoughts. Keep planting positive thoughts in your mind. Do you know that you can listen to positive affirmations, sermons, talks, etc. while sleeping and your subconscious mind will still be taking it in as you sleep? How amazing is that? Make it a habit to surround yourself with positive people and a positive environment. I promise you that you will see a difference in the success in your life if you do.

As I've mentioned early in this book, every morning you are born again to do something great! You have to keep being active to become one day closer to your definite purpose. Move like the clock, FORWARD. Time is so important. Remember that nature gives in abundance. An apple tree does not yield only one apple...please keep that in mind.

BELIEVE that you can accomplish ALL that you set out to do. YOU can't fail. Those so called failures are just setbacks. Yes, those setbacks are stepping stones to success. Those setbacks are practice shots; therefore, you might have setbacks, but you are not defeated.

Let your subconscious mind know that YOU are the boss. Put those thoughts in your mind that will give you YOUR definite purpose. Speak them daily! I must insist though, that you keep your major purpose to yourself. The only way to speak of your definite purpose is through ACTION. If your purpose is to make $100,000 a year, let that be between you and your creator.
You see, if you tell others about your major purpose, more than likely they will discourage you. They will make you feel that the goal is not obtainable.

Those thoughts they share will get into your subconscious mind...and you will begin to have doubts of accomplishing them.

When creating a plan for your definite purpose, you must keep it flexible because you will get intuitions that will let you know to go forward, or to abolish part of the plan. As you proceed, you will understand your plan better.

In general your definite purpose plan should include:

- *That SOMETHING you want to accomplish (e.g. $100,000, new house, new car, business up and running)*

- *Determine WHAT you will give (e.g. good service, more working hours, put money into special account)*

- *Establish a DATE you will accomplish your definite purpose (e.g. by 12/31/20--)*

- *Write a CLEAR STATEMENT including what you will give for the accomplishment of your definite purpose (e.g. the services rendered will be through _____. Rendering these services will easily bring in $100,000. I believe that I will achieve this goal. I can already see the harvest and I embrace it)*

- *READ your STATEMENT at least twice a day, preferably in the morning when you wake and at night, before you go to bed.*

Remember that you have to KNOW your product or service so well that you would buy it yourself. Be sure to ask God for guidance and BELIEVE that He will grant it.

Plan your time, hour by hour. If you work at home, be sure to treat your business as if you are going to the office. It is very easy to procrastinate, because you are not in a work setting that makes you have to follow a schedule. If you are determined to succeed in building and growing your Black Business, you will make your time top priority (at least during business hours).

Part of your time spent developing your business is making people aware of what you are offering as a product or service. Learning marketing skills is a must. Most of the time the marketing part of the business is what people fear the most. People fear rejection, so they hope that someone will just stumble upon their product. Instead, you have to recognize opportunities and act upon them. Don't procrastinate, but attack! Determine where you are going and free your mind of fear and doubt. Let your thoughts be about success, constantly having a CAN DO mentality.

Keep this little saying in the back of your mind. As a matter of fact, hang it on your wall:
"Fear knocks on the door, but FAITH opens it!"

*On this day, whatever day it is...decide to **start now**!*

I can not stress enough the importance of not procrastinating. Let me share a few scriptures on what the bible says about laziness (being a sluggard). Read the following passages below:

Proverbs 6:6 – "Go to the ant, you sluggard! Consider her ways and be wise"

Proverbs 21:25 – "The sluggard's craving will be the death of him, because his hands refuse to work" (he hates to work)

Proverbs 26:14 – "As a door turns on its hinges, so a sluggard turns on his bed" (he loves to sleep)

Proverbs 26:13- "The sluggard says, 'There is a lion in the road, a fierce lion roaming on the streets "(he makes excuses)

Proverbs 18:9 – "He who is slothful in his work is a brother to him who is a great waster" (he wastes time and energy)

Proverbs 26:16 – "The sluggard is wiser in his own eyes than seven men who answer discreetly" (he believes he is wise, but is the fool)

Proverbs 12:24 – "Diligent hands will rule, but laziness ends in slave labor" (a lazy person becomes a servant or debtor)

Proverbs 20:4 – "A sluggard does not plow in season; so at harvest time he looks but finds nothing" (his future is bleak)

Proverbs 13:4 – "The soul of the lazy man desires and has nothing; but the soul of the diligent shall be made rich" (he may come to poverty)

Of course, there are many more scriptures that show us how God feels about laziness and the outcome that befalls those who do nothing. Today, **"decide"** to move forward regardless of the circumstances and/or obstacles.

Another thing that the bible teaches us about business is the "Sowing and the Reaping".
Here are two scriptures that talk about sowing and reaping:

2 Corinthians 9:6 – "But this I say, he which soweth sparingly shall reap also sparingly; and he which soweth bountifully shall reap also bountifully"

Galatians 6:7 – "Be not deceived; God is not mocked: for whatsoever a man soweth, that shall he also reap"

Let us use the previous two scriptures above pertaining to sowing and reaping, and the scripture **Proverbs 6:6 – *"Go to the ant, you sluggard! Consider her ways and be wise"*,** to understand the <u>Ants Philosophy</u>:

Ants never quit *(no matter what obstacles they face, they keep going)*
Ants think winter all summer *(they are always planning for the future)*
Ants think summer all winter *(still they are working hard at planning for their future)*
Ants gather all they possibly can *(they don't make excuses as to why they can carry as much as they can. Heck, they carry loads twice their size!)*

Let me use another illustration of the Sowing and Reaping:

Jesus uses a Parable of the Sower, also known as the Four Soils, which is found in Matthew 13:3-9; Mark 4:2-9; and Luke 8:4-8. I will share **Matthew 13:3-9:**

<u>**Matthew 13:3**</u> **- Then He spoke many things to them in parables saying "Behold, a sower went out to sow.**

<u>**Matthew 13:4**</u>**- And as he sowed, some seed fell by the wayside; and the birds came and devoured them.**

<u>**Matthew 13:5**</u>**- Some fell on stony places, where they did not have much earth; and they immediately sprang up because they had no depth of earth.**

Matthew 13:6- But when the sun was up they were scorched, and because they had no root they withered away.

Matthew 13:7- And some fell among thorns, and the thorns sprang up and choked them.

Matthew 13:8- But others fell on good ground and yielded a crop: some a hundredfold, some sixty, some thirty.

Matthew 13:9- He who has ears to hear, let him hear!"

See the bible verses (Matthew 13:18-23) below that explains the Parable of the Sower.
Please be patient, because after the explanation of the parable meaning, I will show you the business side tied into it.

Matthew 13:18- "Therefore hear the parable of the sower:

Matthew 13:19- When anyone hears the word of the kingdom, and does not understand it, then the wicked one comes and snatches away what was sown in his heart. This is he who received seed by the wayside.
Matthew 13:20- But he who received the seed on stony places, this is he who hears the word and immediately receives it with joy;

Matthew 13:21- Yet he has no root in himself, but endures only for a while. For when tribulation or persecution arises because of the word, immediately he stumbles.

Matthew 13:22- Now he who received seed among the thorns is he who hears the word, and the cares of this world and the deceitfulness of riches choke the word, and he becomes unfruitful.

Matthew 13:23- But he who received seed on the good ground is he who hears the word and understands it, who indeed bears fruit and produces: some a hundredfold, some sixty, some thirty."

Of course, after reading these passages you know that it is intended for "spiritual" understanding. It is all tied into FAITH that is either taken away during hard times, or that has the strength to move forward regardless of the circumstances...which in the end yields increase instead of decrease.

As we study the Sower (The person planting the seed...like a farmer, or some type of business person), let us realize the four qualities that he possesses:

- *He is a wise man*
- *He is ambitious*
- *He is active in what he is trying to get great results*
- *He only plants with excellent seed*

Let's break down the SEED in a business sense:

The SEED falls by the wayside: **Birds are going to get part of the seed. Life disappointments happen. In business, low sales or non-productive employees, etc. Don't spend your time chasing after the birds. Don't leave the field, spend you time on growing, that is, making your crops ready for the harvesting season. **The wise man ignored the birds and kept planting.*

The SEED falls on rocky ground: **It is the stuff of life. The seed started producing plants, but withered. This is a good example of the employees who may only stay days, weeks, etc. Here you have to discipline your disappointment. **The wise man kept planting.*

The SEED falls on thorny ground: **It is inevitable! The seed starts growing, but thorns kill some of the plants. Yes, these are the cares and excuses that come along such as: your employees who have family problems, car trouble, sickness, etc. The employees seem to be growing in their jobs, but somewhere their momentum fades, using excuses as their productivity decreases.*

If you keep them on, they constantly drain you and the business. **The wise man assesses the problem, but keeps on planting.

The SEED falls on good ground: *It always does! You have to be patient, because if you keep on going forward, the reward will pay off!! This is the ground that yields great results by producing a hundredfold, sixty fold, and thirty fold.

The bottom line is that no matter what the circumstances, you MUST keep going and keep doing. **Adopt the Ant Philosophy** of: never quitting, think winter all summer, and think summer all winter. Prepare for the future, don't live only in the now.

In this chapter, I hope I have inspired you to move forward. Create that Black Business! **Start now...**

Chapter 6

Basic Steps to Starting Your Business

As I mentioned in the beginning of this book, this book is not a step by step, start a business book. I will give you an outline of the steps to take to build your Black Business, but not forms, etc. I will share my knowledge and research, hoping to bring you closer to YOUR Black Enterprise.

Please keep in mind, that **no one person has all the answers** for business or anything in general. What may work for one, may not work for the other. If you have been studying business at all, you will find that no two minds think alike. One business book may tell you to do something all together different from what another suggests. The business person normally shares from the experiences they have encountered. Most of the experiences are through trial and error. That said, what I suggest, I hope will be profitable to you. *Please put some research into whatever endeavor you choose to pursue.* No matter what book, seminar or class you take, YOU still have to go the extra mile if you want to be successful in what you are doing.

Sometimes we can read books and watch Ted talks, videos on Youtube, take online classes, etc. and think that we have become an expert. There is always room for improvement and for learning new things. Just remember, *if you are the smartest person in your group, how much can you really be learning?* Therefore, never have the mentality that YOU know it all. Listen and learn from the mentors and people who have sown seeds. There is a saying that says, "Even a broken clock is right twice a day." In order to learn though, you have to listen and meditate on what you learn.

I have a personal philosophy that I believe, "A person can't show you how to do something, if they have never done it themselves".

Therefore, look for the success (or the seeds sown) before taking advice from others. Some people will discourage you from your endeavor, just because they don't want to see your succeed. If a person has no business, they can not tell you how to run a business. If a person has no kids, how can they tell you how to raise them?

On that note, keep in mind that sometimes we assume that we have ALL the answers, or know more than we think we do. Please read the story below entitled "The Cookie Thief" by Valerie Cox. It is humorous, yet fascinating in the message it gives. Read on...

The Cookie Thief

A woman was waiting at an airport one night,
with several long hours before her flight.
She hunted for a book in the airport shops,
bought a bag of cookies and found a place to drop.

She was engrossed in her book but happened to see,
that the man sitting beside her, as bold as could be...
grabbed a cookie or two from the bag in between,
which she tried to ignore to avoid a scene.

So she munched the cookies and watched the clock,
as the gutsy cookie thief diminished her stock.
She was getting more irritated as the minutes ticked by,
thinking, "If I wasn't so nice, I would blacken his eye."

With each cookie she took, he took one too,
when only one was left, she wondered what he would do.
With a smile on his face, and a nervous laugh,
he took the last cookie and broke it in half.

He offered her half, as he ate the other,
she snatched it from him and thought...oooh, brother.

This guy has some nerve and he's also rude,
why he didn't even show any gratitude!

She had never known when she had been so galled,
and sighed with relief when her flight was called.
She gathered her belongings and headed to the gate,
refusing to look back at the thieving ingrate.

She boarded the plane, and sank in her seat,
then she sought her book, which was almost complete.
As she reached in her baggage, she gasped with surprise,
there was her bag of cookies, in front of her eyes.

If mine are here, she moaned in despair,
the others were his, and he tried to share.
Too late to apologize, she realized with grief,
that she was the rude one, the ingrate, the thief.

How many times do we assume something? We feel that our way is right. We have been doing this thing for so long, so why should someone else try to tell us how to do it? True inventors, business people, professionals, etc. don't try to know it all. These people study what other people are doing or have done. They use research and development to either better an existing invention (that solves a problem...need...want), or they create something that hasn't already come to the market, that becomes a solution for a problem. You see, they had to research and learn from others past experiences. I implore you to keep researching and learning throughout your whole business experience. Each year get better. If you are in business five years, ten years, thirty years...keep researching and learning! Why? You have to be the BEST in your industry. Technology, solutions, etc. constantly change. You have to be up to par, to stay in the game.

In the following pages, I will give you a description of the Basic Steps to Starting Your Business. Please keep in mind that different states have different laws, so be sure to check with YOUR state website for additional information (especially when it comes to needing a license for a particular industry).

Shall we begin? Okay, let's **start now...**

By now, I'm sure that you have come up with some ideas of what you would like to bring to the market. Now you have to decide if you will run the business solo (Sole Proprietor), with someone else (Partnership) or create a separate entity from the individual owner or owners (Corporation).

*So, the **first step** is that you have to choose the status of your legal business structure. Which one of the following will you use?*

Sole Proprietorship. *Taking the Sole Proprietor business structure means that you will be the sole owner of the business, and that you are running it completely by yourself (some states extend proprietorship status to your spouse as well). Running your business as sole proprietor, you can hire employees but you have sole legal obligations when it comes to the company.*

Partnership. *Taking the Partnership business structure means two people jointly own the business (they are partners). All partners are equal when it comes to profits and losses. Both partners are also liable for all debts incurred (law suits or losses). Each partner also pays business income taxes based on the percentage of the business they own.*

Corporation. *Taking the Corporation business structure differs from partnership and sole proprietorship for one reason, a corporation is created as a separate entity instead of individual ownership. This means that in case of bankruptcy, assets can't be seized.*

Yes, with the sole proprietorship or partnership you are staking it all on the line because the business is YOU. As a corporation the business is "a separate entity"...therefore, your personal things can't be seized. Only business assets can be liquidated.

Of course, I must mention that taking the corporation business status will cost you a lot more than if you started as a sole proprietor or partnership. It is advised that if your business makes a $1 million or more in profits per year, you may want to consider incorporation.

The **second step**, if you think you may need additional help, is a legal advisor or lawyer. Here is a list of reasons why you might want to consider an advisor (you may not want to start off with one...but just so you know what they can help you with, I have added it):

Helping you establish your business structure
Review of contracts or legal documents prior to signing
Helping with the debt collection process
Helping with law suits or litigations
Advice on dealing with human resource issues (and legal help if necessary)
Advice on leasing agreements (equipment, vehicles, etc.)
Contract matters (whether disputes or understanding them)
Helping you to create legal documents

The **third step**, an accountant, if you need help with your financials. Many business people don't start out with a legal advisor or an accountant, but every business is different...so review your situation and decide if you need extra help. You may want to ask friends and family if they can recommend someone they know. It would be great if you used a Black Business for legal advice or an accountant (if you need these services). Yes, support the Black Businesses in YOUR neighborhood!

Here are a few things that an accountant can help you with:

Tax help (preparing returns and also tax advice)
Preparing your budgets
Preparing financial statements (Balance sheets, Profit and Loss, Cash Flow)
Set up a bookkeeping system for your daily operations
Advise you on budgeting and expenditures

The **fourth step**, whether you skipped step two (legal advisor) or step three (an accountant), you definitely need to choose and register a business name.

If you haven't come up with a name yet, make a list of four or five names you have thought of. Perform searches to see if the name you want is already in use. You will want to search at the local, state and federal levels if you have chosen to be a corporation. This is why deciding your business structure is so important. Several places that you can check to see if the name you want to use is already taken are:

County clerks office
Libraries (which may charge a fee)
Online searches
Trade journals (depending on your industry)

After you have found the right assume name for your business, register it at the county level to ensure that no one can legally use your company's name.

The **fifth step**, apply for a business license. Keep in mind that every state, county, and city has different legal requirements for obtaining a business license. Part of establishing yourself as a business owner is complying with the required laws. You are required by law to comply with local, state and federal regulations.

Therefore, you must register your business to file tax documents. A business license only allows you to operate your business legally in the specified area (or areas).

*The **sixth step**, open a commercial bank account. I'm sure you already know why you need a commercial bank account, but to briefly state it, it is to deposit checks from your clients, pay the business expenses, and basically set up as a legal business financially. Having a commercial account can also help with acquiring credit, and obtaining larger contracts...among other things.*

*The **seventh step**, obtain insurance. Without doubt, liability insurance is a must...no matter what business you are in. It only takes one client to make a claim against you, making it look like your service or product was faulty. Another great factor about liability insurance is that it is inexpensive, and it helps to boost your image as a professional. Of course, if you decide to have employees you will need additional insurance (e.g. Worker's compensation). Depending on your business needs, check into the other types of insurances that might be required for your business.*

Now that we went over the seven steps (above) on starting your business, we need to focus now on developing YOUR plan of action...YOUR BUSINESS PLAN. Whether you are trying to get funding from investors, a bank, etc. or you are starting small, using your own funds...you still need to have a plan to know what you are doing. If you are not trying to get funding, you don't have to have an elaborate plan, but you should still have the basics. The following section is an outline of what your business plan should cover. Don't just guess or copy someone else's plan from online. You need to have goals that will help you meet your "definite purpose" goals. Therefore, do your best...yes, by researching and trial an error. No plan will be set in stone. Throughout the year you will tweak your plan. You will hit some goals on target, and some may be way too high or too low. Adjust your plan as you go along.

WHAT YOUR BUSINESS PLAN SHOULD COVER:

Cover page. You may think you don't need a cover page if you are not trying to get funding, but the cover page serves several purposes. First, it is the place where the location of the business and contact information is displayed. It also warns anyone who may read it, that all information is confidential. If you have a product, visually you can display it on this page.

Table of contents. This section should be as detailed as possible. It should include page numbers for each section.

Executive summary. At this point, you may not feel like an executive, but you have to get the mentality that you are already an executive. In fact, if you are starting a business, you are the executive! I need you to understand this point, because this is the most important section of the business plan. This is where most people start to read, to get a feel of the whole entire plan. In fact, seldom does the investors, etc. read through the whole entire plan...but they always read the executive summary. The executive summary is not an introduction, but is the business plan in a miniature form. It should be able to stand alone as a document. Let's think of it as a business plan inside of the main business plan. When your reader is done reading this part of the plan, they should have a good idea of what your business is all about. Keep in mind that the executive summary should not be more than two pages in length. *I would suggest researching sample executive summaries to get a feel of how you should write yours. Again, I say DO NOT COPY SOMEONE ELSES. Do your homework and it will pay off.

The company. In this section you discuss your company strategy and management team. Keep in mind that since you are beginning a business, your strategy plan will be optimistic until you get a feel of the industry. As far as your management team, this is also an area that will be tweaked as you progress.

Try not to put too much responsibility on a single leader, if you are more than a one man business. When describing your management team, use a paragraph for each team member. Be sure to use everyone's experience and expertise in the descriptions.

The market. You need to know who are the businesses or people who will buy what you are selling. You also need to know how many of them exist in your area, globally if you sell online, etc. This section of the plan identifies your prospects and shows evidence of how many potentially will be candidates to buy from you.

One way to start finding candidates who may fit your marketing criteria is by demographics. Here's an example: Let's say you live in Michigan, and you are a lawn care provider. If you are looking for residential clients, and you are looking for clients in a 30 mile radius from where your business is located...you already have narrowed down the areas you will target. Now you have to also determine who will buy from you.

If you are trying to target residential homes, you will want to look for households that make over $50,000 a year. In these households, the couples both usually work and are buying a house and car, and have no time to keep up the landscaping. You can find information like this in the latest census. You can also find these types of customers in newly developed housing areas.

The product or service. This is the section of the business plan that you might find the easiest to complete. If you feel strongly about your product or service it will come easily to you. When writing this section you must vision the benefits your service or product will be giving to your customers. The benefits that help the customer make money, save money or feel good. Here is an example: If the summer is very hot, the benefit of buying an air conditioning system is the cool air that the client will feel during those extremely hot days.

Sales and promotion. In this section you will explain how sales will be completed. You will explain if you will do the sales, hire a firm or do in-house. You also will explain the different mediums you will use to sale your product or service (direct, online, etc.). What type of promotions will you use? Will you do advertising or public relations? Basically you are explaining your selling approach, and if you are hiring in-house salespeople...how you will motivate them to sell your product.

Finances. In this section three types of financial statements are necessary: cash flow, income/loss, and the balance sheet. You can create these forms easily on Excel or any spreadsheet software program. If you don't understand how to do these forms, search online for some examples. In this section you will be forecasting your financial projections. Experts suggest you have three to five year financial projections. This section should also include your explanation or analysis of the numbers you come up with. If you project losses for a certain period, explain why you feel those losses will occur. Please keep your forms in comply with regular standard financial forms (you want to look as professional as possible). Keep in mind that the **CASH FLOW is the lifeline of the business.** A good way to look at the cash flow is to think of the business as a person. The cash is considered the (food) that feeds the person (business). Without the food (cash) the person (business) can't survive.
*Important to remember...Cash flow is different from profit, and more important for a small business. You see, it is possible to run out of cash and go broke even though you are still making sales that make a profit.
Keep in mind also that cash flow can be used as a planning tool. If you monitor it on a consistent basis as your cash comes in and go out, this will enable you to develop a system to plan for the future.

As for the other two financial statements: the **INCOME STATEMENT is the bottom line of the business.** Here is where the numbers let you know if you have made a profit or a loss.

The BALANCE SHEET is the statement that lets us know the business health. *In this statement it reveals clues such as: the state of assets, liabilities, accounts receivables, etc. at a certain point in time.*

 **If you have problems understanding where to get the information and exactly how to create these forms, as suggested earlier...do some searches online or purchase some business books that will help you understand business processes better.

Appendix. *In this last section you will include items like the executive resumes, product or service literature, and endorsement letters or testimonials from previous clients who have tested your product.*

I hope that this chapter has been of help to you. There is so much to cover in starting and running a business. Even though this chapter is a brief description, I would suggest you download papers, talk to local business owners, find a mentor, and buy books that will help you understand and succeed in whatever your endeavor is. Don't get discouraged or overwhelmed with the lists or suggestions in this chapter. Break it down into bite size steps. If you have to start your business plan on just the executive summary at first, at least you know what YOUR business is about, and what you expect to achieve from it. Start where you feel comfortable, but start now! If you know the assume name you want, make a goal to at least register the name within a week. After you register your name, begin your business plan, even if it is less than 10 pages. Read your plan daily for motivation and direction, until you have it deep down inside of you! Please...start working on your Black Business now.

Chapter 7

Go Forward... (Launch, connect, be an example)

You made it this far...I applaud YOU! As a matter of fact, pat yourself on the back. Many will dream it, but never do it. In this chapter we will talk about **YOU moving forward**. Of course, it is still up to YOU to "**decide**" to do it. Black business is so needed, and YOU can make the difference right in your own neighborhood. I hope to encourage you to KEEP GOING and create something great that will inspire others to get involved too.

No matter what the widget (product/service) is that you are bringing to the market, be proud of what you are doing. As long as it is legal and doesn't harm someone else, you are on the right path.

So far everything probably sounds like there is all happy, and no days of despair in my writing this book. This is not the gloom and doom chapter, but I want to say that not every customer will be an ideal customer, and that you will not be able to satisfy every customer. There are going to be some that no matter what you do, they won't be happy. After you have done all that you can do, it is best to let that customer find the right company for them. I want to encourage you to do the best that you can with every job. That being said though, as just mentioned...some will not fit. Sometimes the chemistry is just not there. Business is about building relationships.

You want the customer to trust you so much, that they will feel confident that you will give a good product or service each and every time. It is sort of like an intimate relationship. What I mean by this, is the trust. Just like you don't want your mate to think every time you walk out the door, that you are being unfaithful...you don't want your customer to expect the worse of your product, and always be looking over your shoulder or checking your product with a fine toothed comb.

Sometimes there can be a misunderstanding at the very beginning. Maybe an order was incomplete, or a product had a defect. One of your employees might have handled a customer service situation different from what you would have, and now the client is irritated. All you can do is try to resolve the issue, but even after that, if the customer doesn't trust you, there will always be disconnect. If so, move on from this situation. **Go forward**, pursuing those customers that will be happy with you and your product. You should learn from the mistake (if you made one), but just remember, sometimes it might not be YOU or YOUR business...it could be the customer. I know it probably sounds contradictory since most say that the customer is always right, but believe me, you can have the customer from outer space! Just remember that YOUR customer is a person. You don't know what type of day they have had, or what circumstances in their living situation could have an affect on their personality. I know that it is no excuse for people to act rudely, but some people wear their emotions on their sleeves. Forgive them, and **go forward**.

There may be times you will be treated unfairly because you are a Black Business. Because of the negative stereotypes associated with Black Business you may be told no, or judged even before you have the chance to prove your product or service. What may surprise you is that the negative stereotypes are often displayed from our own Black people. They often trust a white business, before they will trust a black one. We really have to change that if we want to bring Black wealth into our neighborhoods.

We also need to change that so that our youth can have mentors to look up to. Our youth need to be able to identify with Black people running Black businesses in their neighborhoods. If they don't see it, they may think that we as Black people are suppose to be the customer and not the owner. Please **go forward**, starting in your own neighborhood. **Go forward**, on this mission with me to bring Black wealth into our communities. All it takes is YOUR business, and then another business will come...and then another... Each time one starts, we will be getting closer to that Black wealth! I ask that when YOU are fully in business, please encourage someone else. Be that mentor, even if you can't help financially. Heck, pass this book on, if it will encourage someone else to start their own Black business!

An important factor here is that when a Black business comes into YOUR neighborhood, YOU must buy from it (support it as much as you can). Show the business owner that you are there to support them.

Again, this book is not to put down any other culture. This book is to encourage Black people to get involved in creating their own destination. Yes, don't just dream it...do it! Do it for yourself and your family. Do you recall the scripture in a previous chapter about leaving an inheritance? Here it is again, if you have forgotten:

Proverbs 13:22 – A good man leaveth an inheritance to his children's children

There are many ways to get your business noticed. One way that has worked for me is having my business volunteer at community events (e.g. Make a Difference Day). Joining local associations and getting involved in their events will give your business exposure and give you a chance to network with other businesses. You don't have to join only Black associations, in fact, I discourage it. It is good to be a part of some Black associations, as well as, other business associations that will help you network.

You will find that most business people want to network and share in referring each other. Besides, the bottom line is the "green" dollar bills. We all want to see great sales and a profit. Therefore, network as much as you can, but **do support** black businesses along the way.

As this chapter is entitled "Go Forward"...I want to encourage you to keep going forward on the business journey. No matter what obstacles you may encounter, there is always a solution. Move through the setbacks and still **go forward**! I used the word **Launch** in the title because you need to be encouraged to follow through. Don't just start by taking out the assumed name and creating a business plan. Neither one of these items (assumed name or business plan) will get your business going, if they sit on a shelf or in a drawer. Set weekly goals to keep you focused on the big picture. YOU were made to do YOUR business. Do it now!
I used the word **Connect** also in the title, because it is important for you to connect with other business leaders to keep the momentum (drive) in building and growing your business. You can connect through social networks, local associations...or weekend barbecues! The main point here is to connect with other people who have the business mindset.

I also want to encourage you to BELIEVE so much in what you are doing, that you will **be the example.** I want you to be so proud of what you are doing, that others will see the joy in you. You have to love your business, and enjoy doing it as much as you possibly can. Sure there will be times that you will ask yourself, "Why did I ever start this business?"...but it will be the pleasant customers (and the cash flow) that will make you realize the great opportunity you have been given. Look at each day as a "blessing". You are blessed to be able to do something that you want to do. You are blessed to be able to create something, and actually see it come to fruition. It is so important for you to believe in your product/service. You see, in order for you to sell your widget (product/service) to someone else, they have to see that YOU have confidence in it.

I want you to think of your business as a person. Yes, think of it as your child...something that YOU created. That being said, you know that you have to feed it (customers/cash) in order for it to grow. You also know that you will want to give your child all that you can; therefore, you won't carelessly spend the business money or tarnish its name. Every decision will be based on what is best for the child (business). For example: my business is called Classic Lawncare & Building Maintenance. For short, I call my business CLBM. This is what I call it with every decision I make (e.g. Is this a good decision for CLBM?).

If you are still wondering what your "definite purpose" is... yes, **that thing,** that will make you want to lose sleep over it... I hope that the next chapter will give you more ideas. The next chapter is dedicated to Black inventions and Black business. Be amazed at the talents of the Black people who made a "decision" to keep going...

Chapter 8

Our Forefathers of Inventions and Business

In chapter four, I shared information about a few Black inventors. In this chapter, I want to give more of a lengthy list of inventions and businesses that were created by Black people. I hope that every time you feel discouraged, or just need a boost (a refreshing), that you will come to this chapter for inspiration. To be frank, I'm sure the Forefathers of this chapter often felt like quitting or perhaps, discouraged when the projects weren't going as planned. Keep in mind that they had to do extended research and continuous tweaking until they had a break through. You will have to do the same!

Let me give you the definition of the word Forefathers, because this chapter is dedicated to the black men and women who created the inventions and businesses...passing the torch to us.

Forefathers: *a member of the past generations of one's family or* **people**; *an ancestor*

I love this definition, because it should inspire us as a "people" to unite and build together!

Please keep in mind that the inventions and businesses of the following Black people have helped to make our world a better place. I stress this whether you are from America, Africa, Haiti, etc. **Our people have made significant input in the development of health, science, engineering, countries, and lands...the world!** I want to stress that we need to celebrate "OUR GREATNESS" everyday...instead of just February (Black History Month).

62

<u>We make HISTORY everyday.</u> ***This chapter is dedicated to ALL black people who have created an invention or business, no matter what land. Hats off to YOU!**

Shall we begin? Ok, let's start now...

In this chapter, you will discover that it was a Black person who created the Street sweeper truck, the rotary-blade lawn mower, long-distance flight airplane, HVAC systems, first super computer, Super Soaker water gun, designed the first programmable ROM cartridge-based video game console, and designed the gas mask, the traffic signal, security surveillance system and much, much more. Keep reading!

The following list is taken from Wikipedia entitled "List of African-American Inventors and Scientists" (http://en.wikipedia.org/wiki/List_of_African-American_inventors_and_scientists). Please see chapter 10 (Appendix/references) of this book for the references.

Harold Amos (1918 – 2003) – Microbiologist
- First African-American department chair at Harvard Medical School (ref. 5)

George Edward Alcom, Jr. (1940 -) – Physicist, inventor
- Invented a method of fabricating an imaging X-ray spectrometer (ref. 6,7)

James J. Andrews (1930 – 1998) – Mathematician
- Put forth the Andrews-Curtis conjecture in group theory with Morton L. Curtis, still unsolved (ref. 8)

Archie Alexander (1888 – 1958) – Civil engineer
- Responsible for the construction of many roads and ridges, including the Whitehurst Freeway, the Tidal Basin Bridge, and an extension to the Baltimore-Washington Parkway.

***Leonard C. Bailey** (? – 1918) – Inventor*
- Folding bed (ref. 9)

***Alice Augusta Ball** (1892 – 1916) – Chemist*
- Extracted chaulmoogra oil for the treatment of Hansen's disease (leprosy)   (ref. 10)

***Benjamin Banneker** (1731 – 1806) – Mathematician, astronomer, surveyor, clockmaker, author, farmer*
- Wooden clock (1753); assisted in survey of the original boundaries of the District of Columbia (1791); authored almanac and ephemeris (1792-1797)   (ref. 11)

***Augustin Banyaga** (1947 -) - Mathematician*
- Work on diffeomorphisms and symplectomorphisms (ref. 12)

***Janet Bashen** (1957 -) – Inventor, entrepreneur, professional, consultant*
- First African-American woman to receive a patent for a web-based software invention, LinkLine, an Equal Opportunity case management and tracking software (ref. 13)

***Patricia Bath** (1942 -) – Ophthalmologist*
- First African-American female physician to receive a patent for a medical invention; inventions relate to cataract surgery and include the Laserphaco Probe, which revolutionized the industry in the 1980's, and an ultrasound technique for treatment (ref. 14, 15, 16)

***Andrew Beard** (1849 – 1921) – Farmer, carpenter, blacksmith, railroad worker, businessman, inventor*
- Janney coupler improvements; invented the car device #594,059 dated November 23, 1897; rotary engine patent #478,271 dated July 5, 1892 (ref. 17)

Earl S. Bell *(1977 -) – Inventor, entrepreneur, architect, industrial designer*
- Invented chair with sliding skin (2004) and the quantitative display apparatus (2005)   (ref. 18, 19, 20)

Miriam Benjamin *(1861 – 1947) – Inventor, educator*
- Invented "Gong and Signal Chair for Hotels"; second African-American woman to receive a patent (ref. 21)

Leonidas Berry *(1902 – 1995) – Gastroenterologist*
- Gastroscope pioneer *(ref. 22)*

Albert T. Bharucha-Reid *(1927 – 1985) – Mathematician, statistician*
- Probability theory and Markov chain theorist (ref. 23)

Keith Black *(1957 -) – Neurosurgeon*
- Brain tumor surgery and research (ref. 24, 25)

David Blackwell *(1919 – 2010) – Mathematician, statistician*
- First proposed the Blackwell channel model used in coding theory and information theory; one of the eponyms of the Rao-Blackwell theorem, which is a process that significantly improves crude statistical estimators (ref. 26)

Henry Blair *(1807 – 1860) – Inventor*
- Second black inventor to issue a patent; invented seed planter and cotton planter (ref. 27, 28)

Kwabena Boahen *(1964 -) – Bioengineer*
- Silicon retina able to process images in the same manner as a living retina (ref. 29, 30)

Sarah Boone *(1832 – 1905) – Inventor*
- Ironing board allowing sleeves of women's garments to be ironed more easily (ref. 31, 32, 33)

Edward Bouchet *(1852 – 1918) – Physicist*
- First African-American to receive a Ph.D. in any subject; received physics doctorate from Yale University in 1876

James Bowman *(1923 – 2011) – Physician*
- Pathologist and geneticist; Professor Emeritus Pritzker School of Medicine; first tenured African-American professor at the University of Chicago Division of Biological Sciences (ref. 34, 35)

Otis Boykin *(1920 – 1982) – Inventor, engineer*
- Artificial heart pacemaker control unit (ref. 36, 37, 38)

St. Elmo Brady *(1884 – 1966) – Chemist*
- Published three scholarly abstracts in Science; collaborated on a paper published in the Journal of Industrial and Engineering Chemistry (ref. 39)

Herman Branson *(1914 – 1995) Physicist, educator*
- Protein structure research (ref. 40, 41)

Charles Brooks *(1865 - ?) Inventor*
- Street sweeper truck and a type of paper punch

Phil Brooks *(19xx -) Inventor*
- First US patent for a disposable syringe

Henry Brown *(1832 - ?) Inventor*
- Invented fire safe (ref. 42)

Oscar E. Brown *(18xx - ?) Inventor*
- Received a patent for an improved horseshoe (ref. 43)

John Albert Blurr *(18xx - ?) Inventor*
- Rotary-blade lawn mower patent (ref. 44)

Thomas C. Cannon *(1943 -) Inventor*
- Led a group of engineers who developed the Tactical Optical Fiber Connector (TOFC), the first fiber optic connector deployed under battlefield conditions, and the ST Connector that helped make fiber optic communications affordable.

William P. Cardozo *(1905 – 1962) Pediatrician*
- Sickle cell anemia studies; in October 1937 he published "Immunologic Studies in Sickle Cell Anemia: in the Archives of Internal Medicine; many of the findings are still valid today

Ben Carson *(1951 -) Pediatric neurosurgeon*
- Pediatric neurosurgery at Johns Hopkins University; first surgeon to successfully separate craniopagus twins (ref. 45)

George Washington Carver *(1865 – 1943) Botanical researcher*
- Discovered hundreds of uses for previously useless vegetables and fruits, principally the peanut (ref. 1, 46, 47, 48, 49)

Charles W. Chappelle *(1872 – 1941) Electrician, construction, international businessman, and aviation pioneer*
- Designed long-distance flight airplane; the only African-American to invent and display the airplane at the 1911 First Industrial Air Show held in conjunction with the Auto Show at Grand Central Palace in Manhattan in New York City; president of the African Union Company, Inc. (ref. 50, 51, 52)

Emmett Chappelle *(1925 -) Scientist and researcher*
- Valuable contributions to several fields; medicine, biology, food science, and astrochemistry

Mamie Clark *(1914 – 2005) Psychologist*
- Conducted 1940's experiments using dolls to study children's attitudes about race

Kenneth Clark *(1917 – 1983) Psychologist*
- First Black president of the American Psychological Association (ref. 53)

David Crosthwait, Jr. *(1898 – 1976) Research engineer*
- Heating, ventilation, and air conditioning; received some 40 US patents relating to HVAC systems

James H (Nick) Curtis *(1935 -) Researcher, chemist (electronics/specialty chemicals)*
- Organic ionogen for aluminum electrolytic capacitors, cationic dialdehyde polysaccharides for wet strength paper and others, US Patent Office US Pat #3609467 US Pat #3547423

John Dabiri *(1980 -) Biophysicist*
- Expert on jellyfish hydrodynamics and designer of the vertical-axis wind farm adapted from schooling fish

Marie Maynard Daly *(1921 – 2003) Chemist*
- First black American woman with a PH.D. in chemistry

Mark Dean *(1957 -) Computer scientist*
- Led the team that developed the ISA bus, and led the design team responsible for creating the first one-gigahertz computer processor chip (ref. 54, 55, 56)

Charles Drew *(1904 – 1950) Medical researcher*
- Developed improved techniques for blood storage

Paul Du Chaillu *(1831 – 1903) Zoologist, Explore, Anthropologist*
- Explorer, first modern European outsider to confirm the existence of gorillas, and later the Pygmy people of central Africa; identified as white throughout his life, but his mother was a Reunionnais mulatto; settled in America and considered it his country by adoption; the full aspects of his ancestry were not uncovered until 1979, and are still little known today

Annie Easley *(1933 – 2011) Computer scientist*
- Work at the Lewis Research Center of the National Aeronautics and Space Administration and its predecessor, the National Advisory Committee for Aeronautics (ref. 57, 58, 59)

Clarence "Skip" Ellis *(1943 -) Computer scientist*
- First African American with a PH.D. in computer science; software inventor including Office Talk at Xerox PARC (ref. 60,61)

Bisi Ezerioha *(1972 -) Automotive engineer*
- Drag racing engineer and driver

Lloyd Noel Ferguson (1918 – 2011) *Chemist, educator*
- Chemistry doctorate, first received (1943, University of California, Berkeley)   (ref. 62, 63, 64)

Roland G. Fryer, Jr. (1977 -) *Economist, social scientist, statistician*
- Inequality studies

Sylvester James Gates (1950 -) *Theoretical physicist*
- Work on supersymmetry, supergravity, and superstring theory (ref. 65,66)

Sarah E. Goode (1855 – 1905) *Inventor*
- Cabinet bed invention; first African-American woman to receive a patent in the United States (ref. 67, 68)

Juan E. Gilbert (1969 -) *Computer scientist*
- Awarded the first Presidential Endowed Chair at Clemson University in honor of his accomplishments

George F. Grant (1846 – 1910) *Dentist, Professor*
- The first African-American professor at Harvard, Boston dentist, and inventor or a wooden golf tee (ref. 69)

Joseph L. Graves (1955 -) *Evolutionary biologist* (ref. 70, 71, 72)

Kevin Greenaugh (1956 -) *Nuclear engineer* (ref. 73)

Bessie Blout Griffin (1914 – 2009) *Physical therapist, inventor*
- Amputee self-feeding device (ref. 74, 75)

Lloyd Hall (1894 -1971) *Chemist*

James A. Harris (1932 – 2000)
- Co-discovered Rutherfordium (element 104) and Dubnium (element 105) at Lawrence Livermore Laboratory (ref. 76)

Walter Lincoln Hawkins (1911 – 1992) *Scientist*
- Inventor at Bell Laboratories (ref. 77)

John E. Hodge (1914 – 1996) *Chemist*

Kerrie Holley (1954 -) *Research computer scientist at IBM*
- Co-creator of Service-Oriented Modeling and Architecture, SOMA and the Service Integration Maturity Model (SIMM)

Mary Jackson (1921 – 2005) *Mathematician, Aerospace engineer*
- NASA's first black female engineer

Erich Jarvis (19xx -) *Neurobiologist*
- Duke University neuroscience bird songs studies (ref. 78, 79, 80)

Issac Johnson (18xx - ?) *Inventor*
- Held patent for improvements to the bicycle frame, specifically so it could be taken apart for compact storage (ref. 81)

Lonnie Johnson (1949 -) *Mechanical engineer, nuclear engineer, inventor*
- Invented Super Soaker while researching thermal energy transfer engines; worked with NASA; holder of over 80 patents (ref. 2, 3, 4, 82, 83, 84)

Oluwabusuyi Isola (1965 -) *Professor, International Finance, inventor*
- Invented Double Sided Guitar

Katherine Johnson (1918 -) *Physicist, Mathematician*
- Made contributions to the United States' aeronautics and space programs with the early application of digital electronic computers at NASA

Frederick McKinley Jones (1893 – 1961) *Inventor*
- Invented refrigerated truck systems (ref. 85)

Percy Julian (1899 – 1975) *Chemist*
- First to synthesize the natural product physostigmine; earned 130 chemical patents; lauded for humanitarian achievements (ref. 86, 87, 88, 89)

Ernest Just (1883 -1941) *Woods Hole Marine Biology Institute biologist*
- Provided basic and initial descriptions of the structure-function-property relationship of the plasma membrane of biological cells (ref. 90, 91, 92)

Rick Kittles (1967 -) *Geneticist*
- Work in tracing the ancestry of African Americans via DNA testing (ref. 93, 94)

Samuel L. Kountz (1930 – 1981) *Transplant surgeon, researcher*
- Organ transplantation pioneer, particularly renal transplant research and surgery; author or coauthor of 172 articles in scientific publications (ref. 95, 96, 97, 98)

Lewis Latimer (1848 – 1928) *Inventor, draftsman, expert witness*
- Worked as a draftsman for both Alexander Graham Bell and Thomas Edison; became mentor of Edison's Pioneers and served as an expert witness in many light bulb litigation lawsuits; said to have invented the water closet (ref. 99, 100, 101, 102)

Jerry Larson (1940 – 2011) *Computer engineer*
- Designer of Fairchild Channel F, the first programmable ROM cartridge-based video game console (ref. 103, 104)

Raphael Carl Lee (1949 -) *Surgeon, biomedical engineer*
- Paul and Aileen Russell Professor, Pritzker School of Medicine; MacArthur Fellow, Searle Scholar, founder and Chairman, Avocet Polymer Technologies, Inc.; founder and Chairman, Renacyte BioMolecular Technologies, Inc; discovered use of surfactant copolymers as molecular chaperones to augment endogenous injury repair mechanisms of living cells; holder of many patents covering scar treatment therapies, tissue engineered ligaments, brain trauma therapies, and protective garments

Beebe Steven Lynk (1972 – 1948) *Chemist*
- Teacher at West Tennessee University

Mary Mahoney (1845 – 1926) *Nurse*
- First African American to study and work as a professionally trained nurse in the United States (ref. 105)

Jan Matzeliger (1852 – 1889) *Inventor*
- Shoe assembly Machine (ref. 106, 107)

Henry McBay (1914 – 1995) *Chemist*
- His discoveries allowed chemists around the world to create inexpensive peroxide compounds (ref. 108, 109)

Elijah McCoy (1844 – 1929) I*nventor*
- Invented a version of the automatic lubricator for steam engines, McCoy learned a great deal of his skills from a mechanical apprenticeship when he was age fifteen (ref. 110, 111)

James McLurkin (1972 -) *Roboticist* (ref. 112)

John McWhorter (1965 -) *Linguist*
- Specializes in the study of creole language formation

Benjamin Montgomery (1819 – 1877) *Inventor*
- Designed a steam operated propeller to provide propulsion to boats in shallow water

Willie Hobbs Moore (1934 – 1994) *Physicist*
- First African American woman to earn a Ph.D. in Physics (University of Michigan Ann Arbor 1972) on vibrational analysis of secondary chlorides (ref. 113)

Thomas Mensah (1950 -) *Inventor*

Murphy Nmezi (1955 -) *Physician/biostatistician*
- Advances in path analysis and structural equation modeling

Jerome Nriagu (1944 -) *Geochemist*
- Studies toxic metals in the environment; supporter of the lead poisoning thesis of the decline of the Roman Empire

John Uzo Ogbu (1939 – 2003) *Anthropologist*
- Ethnic studies in education and economics (ref. 114, 115)

Kunle Olukotun (19xx -) *Computer scientist*
- Early advocate and researcher of multi-core processors

Soni Oyekan (1946 -) *Chemical engineer*
- Inventions in oil refining

Hildrus Poindexter (1901 – 1987) *Bacteriologist, epidemiologist*
- Work on the epidemiology of tropical diseases, including malaria

Arlie Petters (1964 -) *Physicist*
- Work on the mathematical physics of gravitational lensing

Lloyd Albert Quarterman (1918 – 1982) *Scientist, fluoride chemist*
- Manhattan Project, worked with Albert Einstein and Enrico Fermi

Earl Renfroe (1907 – 2000) *Orthodontist* (ref. 116, 117)

Norbert Rillieux (1806 – 1894) *Engineer, inventor*
- Inventor of the multiple-effect evaporator (ref. 118)

Larry Robinson (1957 -) *Environmental chemist*
- Investigated possible role of arsenic in the death of Zachary Taylor; interim president of Florida A & M University

Jesse Russell (1948 -) *Engineer, inventor*
- Wireless communications engineer

Walter Sammons (1890 – 1973) *Inventor*
- Patent for hot comb (ref. 119)

Thomas Sowell (1930 -) *Economist, social scientist*
- Economist, social theorist and political philosopher (ref. 120, 121, 122, 123)

Claude Steele (1946 -) *Psychologist, social scientist*
- Stereotype threat studies

Lee Stiff (1941 -) *Mathematician*
- President of the National Council of Teachers of Mathematics from 2000 to 2002 (ref. 124)

Window Snyder (1976 -) *Computer engineer*
- Security engineer at Microsoft, Mozilla, and Apple

Lewis Temple (1800 – 1854) *Inventor, blacksmith, abolitionist*
- Inventor of the toggling whaling harpoon head (ref. 125)

Vivien Thomas (1910 – 1985) *Surgical technician*
- Blue baby syndrome treatment in the 1940s (ref. 126, 127, 128)

Charles Henry Turner (1867 – 1923) *Zoologist*
- First person to prove that insects can hear and can distinguish pitch, that cockroaches can learn by trial and error, and that honeybees can see color; first African-American to receive a Ph.D. from the University of Chicago (ref. 129)

Bernadette G. Tyree (19xx -) *Biochemist*
- Program Director, Division of Musculoskeletal Diseases, at National Institute of Arthritis and Musculosketetal and Skin Diseases, National Institutes of Health (ref. 130)

Neil deGrasse Tyson (1958 -) *Astronomer*
- Researcher and popular educator in astronomy and the sciences (ref. 131, 132, 133)

Dorothy Vaughan (1910 – 2008) *Mathematician*
- Worked for NACA and NASA at Langley Research Center

Powtawche Valerino (1980) *Engineer*
- Worked for JPL and NASA at Langley Research Center

Arthur B. C. Walker, Jr. (1936 – 2001) *Astronomer*
- Developed normal incidence multilayer XUV telescopes to photograph the solar corona (ref. 134, 135, 136)

C. J. Walker (1867 – 1919) *Inventor*
- Created black cosmetic products

Warren M. Washington (1936 -) *Atmospheric scientist*
- Former chair of the National Science Board (ref. 137, 138, 139, 140)

James E. West (1931 -) *Acoustician, inventor*
- Co-developed the foil electret microphone (ref. 141, 142, 143)

J. Ernest Wilkins Jr. (1923 – 2011) *Mathematician, engineer, nuclear scientist*
- Entered University of Chicago at age 13; Ph.D. at 19; worked on the Manhattan Project; wrote over 100 scientific papers; helped recruit minorities into the sciences (ref. 144, 145, 146)

Daniel Williams (1856 – 1931) *Surgeon*
- The first black person on record to have successfully performed pericardium (the sac surrounding the heart) surgery to repair a wound (ref. 147)

Scott W. Williams (1943 -) *Mathematician*

Walter E. Williams (1936 -) *Economist, social scientist* (ref. 148, 149, 150)

Granville Woods (1856 – 1910) *Inventor*
- Invented the synchronous multiplex railway telegraph (ref. 151)

Jane C. Wright (1919 – 2013) *Cancer research and surgeon*
- Noted for her contributions to chemotherapy and for pioneering the use of the drug methotrexate to treat breast cancer and skin cancer

Louis T. Wright (1891 – 1952) *Surgeon*
- Led team that first used Aureomycin as a treatment on humans (ref. 152, 153, 154)

Roger Arliner Young (1899 – 1964) *Zoologist*
- First African-American woman to receive a doctorate degree in zoology (ref. 155, 156)

The following information is taken from the website: http://thinkgrowth.org/14-black-inventors-you-probably-didnt-know-about-3c0702cc63d2 14 Black Inventors You Probably Didn't Know About by: Pamela Rosario Perez (Feb. 26, 2017)

(1) **Dr. Shirley Jackson** (1946 – Present) *Theoretical Physicist*
Shirley is an American physicist who received her Ph.D. in 1973 from the Massachusetts Institute of Technology.

She was the first African-American woman to earn a doctorate in nuclear physics at MIT. Her experiments with theoretical physics paved the way for numerous developments in the telecommunications space including the touch-tone telephone, the portable fax, called ID, call waiting, and the fiber-optic cable. Today, she is the 18th president of Rensselaer Polytechnic Institute in Troy, New York.

(2) **Lewis Latimer** (1848 – 1928) *Inventor and Draftsman*
Lewis was born in Chelsea, Massachusetts, on September 4, 1848. He collaborated with the science greats such as: Thomas Edison and Hiram Maxim. One of his greatest inventions was the carbon filament, which was a vital component of the light bulb. Besides the above accomplishment, he worked with Alexander Graham Bell. He helped draft the patent for Bell's design of the telephone. Lewis also designed an improved railroad car bathroom and an early air conditioning system.

(3) **Marie Van Brittan Brown** (1922 – 1999) *Inventor*
I bet you didn't know that the first home security system was invented by a Black nurse! Although she was a full-time nurse, she recognized the security threats to her home and devised a system that would alert her of strangers at her door and contact relevant authorities as quickly as possible. Marie's original invention consisted of peepholes, a camera, monitors, and a two-way microphone. The finishing touch was the alarm button...when pressed, would alert the authorities (police). Her patent laid the groundwork for the modern closed-circuit television system that is widely used for surveillance, home security systems, push-button alarm triggers, crime prevention, and traffic monitoring.

(4) **Otis Boykin** (1920 – 1982) *Inventor*
Otis was known for his circuit improvements he made to pacemakers after losing his mother to heart failure.
He had 26 patents in his name. Among his inventions, he is known for developing IBM computers, burglar-proof cash registers, chemical air filters, and the electronic resistor used in controlled missiles, and other devices.

(5) **Lonnie G. Johnson** (1949 – Present) *Aerospace engineer*
Lonnie is the known for creating the most famous water gun. He made the Super Soaker. He isn't a toymaker, but yet, a Aerospace Engineer for NASA with credentials such as: boasting a stint with the US Air Force, work on the Galileo Jupiter probe and Mars Observer project, and is responsible for more than 40 patents. He is also working on the Johnson Thermoelectric Energy Converter (JTEC) which converts heat directly into electricity.

(6) **Charles Drew** (1904 – 1950) *Physician and Medical Researcher*
Charles was a physician, surgeon, and medical researcher who worked with a team at the Red Cross on break through discoveries that surrounded blood transfusions. He played a major role in developing the first large-scale blood banks and blood plasma programs. He also invented the bloodmobiles. The bloodmobiles are the refrigerated trucks that (even until this day) transport stored blood to locations that need it. Charles was a pioneer, a true leader to be recognized because he was one of the most prominent doctors working in his field, especially during a period when blood donation was still separated along lines of race. He eventually resigned from his position with the Red Cross over their insistence on adhering to policy. It wasn't until 1950 that the Red Cross finally recognized all blood as being equal.

(7) **Marian R. Croak** - *SVP, AT&T LABS*
Marian was inducted into the Women in Technology International's hall of fame in 2013. She holds over 135 patents, primarily in voice over Internet protocol (VoIP), and some in other areas. Would you believe she has another 100 patents currently under review? Wow! Now that is extraordinary! Marian is currently SVP at AT&T, serves as a mentor for women in AT&T labs, and sits on the board for the Holocaust, Genocide and Human Rights Education Center.

(8) **Lisa Gelobter** – *VP, BET*
Lisa was involved in the advent of Shockwave, a technology that formed the beginning of web animation. She also played a major role in the emergence of online video, and later serving on the senior management team at Hulu. She previously was the Interim Head of Digital for BET Networks and ran Technology, Product and Business Operations. Currently, she is at the White House, in the United States Digital Service. She is currently serving as the Chief Digital Service Officer with the US Department of Education.

(9) **Philip Emeagwali** (1954 – Present) *Scientist*
Philip was forced to drop out of school at age 14 because of the cost. Being a drop out didn't keep him from becoming one of the greatest computer pioneers of our time. To be frank, he is often called "The Bill Gates of Africa." In his adult years, he began studying nature, specifically bees. The construction of the honeycombed inspired him to rethink computer processing. In 1989, he put his idea to work, using 65,000 processes to invent the world's first super computer. The computer was able to perform 3.1 billion calculations per second. A true genius!

(10)   **Jesse Earnest Wilkins, Jr.** (1923 – 2011)
Mathematician
Jesse is one of America's most important contemporary mathematicians. He became the University of Chicago's youngest student at age 13. He continued his studies there, earning a bachelor, master, and eventually earning his doctorate degree in mathematics at the age of 19. He is credited for publishing papers in mathematics, optics, and nuclear engineering.

(11)   **Elijah McCoy** (1843 – 1929) *Inventor*
Elijah was credited for 50 inventions over the span of his career. He devised a method that would eliminate the frequent stopping that was necessary for the lubricating of the trains. His method was the "lubricating cup" that he developed in 1872. This invention would automatically drip oil when and where needed, which was vital in avoiding sticking to the tracks. The lubricating cup was so popular that railroad companies all over the country order it. It was also so popular that when other inventors tried to steal the idea, the companies weren't fooled…and they demanded the authentic device, calling it "The Real McCoy."

(12)   **Garrett Morgan** (1877 – 1963) *Inventor*
Garrett was the first to create the "safety hood" to help firefighters navigate in smokey buildings, later modifying it to carry its own air supply…making it the world's first effective gas masks. He was also the clever one who added a third position to the traffic signal. At first, the traffic signal was only "stop or go", but his addition "caution light" reduced automobile accidents.

(13)   **Mary and Mildred Davidson** – *Inventors*
Mary and her sister Mildred patented many practical inventions.

Neither of them had technical education, but they were exceptional at finding ways to make peoples' lives better. Together they invented the sanitary belt. Later, Mary invented the moisture-resistant pocket for the belt. While she was disabled from multiple sclerosis, Mary went on to invent the walker and the toilet-tissue holder.

I hope that this chapter has been informative to you. Whenever you need a boost of confidence, refer back to this chapter. It is remarkable to see for example: A Black nurse (Marie Van Brittan Brown) invent a security system. Whoever said we could only be good at one thing? Remember my little saying "Keep going"... **_YOU have what it takes_**_!_ **Let this chapter be your motivation.**

Chapter 9

Diane Thomas-Newbill...the Author

The goal of this book is to "inspire you" to start a Black Business in YOUR Community. Even though I have shared a few ideas on things you could do, and how to get your business started...the main focus is to get YOU to "decide" to **start yours now...**

Though this chapter is entitled "Diane Thomas-Newbill...the Author", it is really a chapter about my experiences and beliefs that I want to share with you. Of course, you have a right to agree or disagree with my beliefs. The bottom line is that YOU have to make a decision to keep going forward. Today, I pass the torch to YOU.

I would like for you (the reader) to take the time to rate this book on Amazon. I hope that it will be a book you will share with someone else, and that it will encourage you to go beyond your own boundaries. Fear is the thing that keeps us from trying...from moving forward. We have the fear of failing, the fear of being rejected, the fear of not being good enough...and yes, the fear that someone will criticize us. With all of those fears lurking in the dark, how can we possibly keep going? My answer: Just remember that everyday you are **blessed** with another day to do and be something great. Of course, as I have said many times in this book...it is up to YOU to "**decide**". Keep in mind that whatever you choose, you have made a decision (to do or not to do something).

My definition of the two words **NICE** and **KIND** in business:

Most people look at these two words and think that they really mean the same thing. I look at these words and I say that they are totally different in meaning. I see the word NICE as objects, and the word KIND associated with people.

My whole philosophy (Diane's philosophy) is that in business I want NICE things such as: nice amount of money, nice house, nice car, and nice clothes, nice... In order for me to get those NICE things, I have to have the right mindset. I have to treat people with kindness. Those people consist of: employees, co-workers, clients, society, etc. Through showing that kindness, even at times when the other person may not, I will yield the things (NICE things) that I want. Part of that kindness is giving great service. Great service is not just the product itself, but the whole package...the experience that the customer comes away with. The same is true if you are going on a job interview or trying to obtain a new client to serve. What is the other person's impression or experience from dealing with you? Understand the difference between these two words (NICE and KIND) and you will see business in a whole new way.

I mentioned the two words above, because they not only affect business, but your personal life as well. The impact YOU can make on your community has to do with your mindset, and everyone else's in that environment. We hear the expression "Black lives matter" and they really do! No one should have to lose their life over senseless things, or feel that they are inferior to any other type of people. This is where the Black Business aspect can help. Of course, my little part here won't change the world, but hopefully "start" a process of building us up. Hand in hand, we need to grab that torch and begin our race to Black Wealth. Sure you may feel that YOU can't do it, but I assure you...YOU CAN! We need to see the Black presence of Black Businesses in our neighborhoods again.

When I was a little girl, I lived in Romulus, Michigan. Of course, back then there were dirt roads and country living. As I reflect back on my childhood days, I remember the local party store that was owned by a Black man named Mr. Jones. Mr. Jones knew us by name, shared some of his stories, sold us and also gave us penny candy. He made you feel welcomed when you came in his store. He also would scold you with his stern words, if he saw you doing something wrong. All the children respected him.

As a matter of fact, the children respected the elders in the community. If you didn't respect the elders, your parents would find out about it.

The neighborhood was like a big family. If your next door neighbor saw you doing something wrong, they would say something to you, and you would respect them as if they were your parents. Nowadays people are afraid to say anything if they see something going wrong. They have the fear of the parent confronting them, the fear of the child cursing them out, or the fear of some type of violence occurring. We need to care enough as a "People" to want the best for our youth…and for each other. Let's take back our neighborhoods by first respecting and loving each other again. We have enough enemies out there without being "our own" enemies. Second, let us "build" Black wealth by creating Black enterprises in our neighborhoods that our youth can remember, and in years to come…continue. Lastly, let us remember that in building our businesses and neighborhoods, we are "lifting each other up" and not tearing each other down. **We will celebrate every business and neighborhood that comes up (improves/grows)!**

When I grew up in Romulus, I remember the Black influence of teachers, neighbors, police, gas stations, the library (which I visited often), the ice cream dairy that had an arcade, and much more. I remember being safe in the neighborhood and racing home before the street lights came on. I keep stressing the neighborhood, because I honestly felt safe. The kids of the neighborhood were like family. We would make tents in our back yards and camp out. Things have changed so much, but we need to bring back the "safety" to our children and grandchildren. I don't say the following to offend anyone who is in the music industry, but we need to write songs that encourage instead of degrading. We need to be the positive influence, which is why I will continuously say that *"Black children need to know how to make money in an honest way and how to save and spend wisely at the earliest age possible"*.

A little about myself:
If you have read this book, you have already learned quite a bit about me. I love people! I feel blessed to be in this world and most of all...I love God! I feel that we were all born to do something great!

In this lifetime, I have worked various jobs (fast food, manufacturing, general maintenance, janitorial, librarian, paraprofessional, business owner, writer/author...and best of all...wife, parent and grandparent).

My mind is always thinking. I suppose I would be called "God's terrible two", because I just can't stop and won't stop! Over the years, I have run several businesses. I have run a secretarial business, a web design business, and a janitorial business. I have worked as a leasing agent, janitor, grounds woman and maintenance woman at Apartment complexes. I was the Management Development Vice President of the Ypsilanti Jaycees, and even a Boy Scout leader in our neighborhood. I currently have been running my own business since 1998. In 2007, I combined two businesses together which is called "Classic Lawncare & Building Maintenance". For short... and as a person, I call my business CLBM. Our business has two websites: http://www.clbm.net and http://www.classiclawncarebuildingmaintenance.com. The clbm.net website is our "social side" and the classiclawncarebuildingmaintenance.com website is our official business website. I encourage you to visit our websites to get a feel of what we are all about. I also encourage you to drop me a note if you have any business questions, or want to share what your enterprise is about. Drop me a note at: dianenewbill@live.com.

In closing this chapter, I want to encourage you again to move forward on researching and starting your own Black Business. *Please also support the Black Businesses in your neighborhoods. Let them know that you are happy they are there.*

I also want to encourage you to be the best that YOU can be. Never stop improving yourself! I personally have a bucket list that I am trying to complete. Just in the last year, I became ordained as a minister, bought an electric guitar and take online guitar lessons, and I bought a very small programming computer called a Raspberry Pi...that I'm learning to use for programming. Keep reaching...keep going...never quit. **Each day challenge yourself to be better than the day before!**

Besides running a lawn and building maintenance business, being ordained, and playing the electric guitar horribly (lol!). I truly love writing. I have previously written books in the fiction, fantasy, religion and children genres. See the list below:
1. **The Man Across the Street**
2. **On the Playground**
3. **Painted Lady** (First book of a series entitled "The Family")
4. **Valiant Man** (Second book of series entitled "The Family")
5. **A Passionate Life** (Third book of series entitled "The Family")
6. **Leading and Loving You** (Fourth book of series entitled "The Family")
7. **My Sister Adah** (Fifth book of series entitled "The Family")
8. **My Brother Asher** (Sixth book of the series entitled "The Family")
9. **The Black Angel ******

Lastly, but not least...I have four wonderful children (Clinton L. Thomas, Timothy D. Thomas, Matthew L. Thomas and Sharonda L. Thomas), and six adorable grandchildren (Trevonte, Clinton Jr., Timothy, Kayla, LaNaysha, and Shakira). ***To you...I dedicated this book and pass the torch!*** **Yes, I only expect excellence. You were born to be great!**

To everyone who reads this book: Thank you and may you be blessed and inspired to start YOUR own Black Business!
I salute you!
Diane Thomas-Newbill

Chapter 10

Appendix (References and Resources)

Appendix A. – References:

In the "Introduction" section of this book, THE POWER OF BUSINESS OWNERSHIP information was taken from the 2012 Census Bureau and http://www.Blackdemographics.com

*ALL SCRIPTURES WERE TAKEN FROM THE HOLY BIBLE.

In Chapter 3, "Goals and Stereotypes of Black Business", the GOALS FOR AFRICAN-AMERICAN BUSINESSES information was taken from the http://www.USBlackchamber.org.

In Chapter 4, "Born to Create and Develop...A history to be proud of", the information pertaining to Garrett Morgan, Lewis Latimer, Thomas Elkins, Benjamin Banneker, Philip Emeagwali, Frederick Jones, Daniel Hale Williams, Alexander Miles and Patricia Bath was taken from the Congressional Black Caucus Foundation/The Village: http://www.cbcfinc.org/thevillage/2015/02/27/top-ten-black-inventors-you-didnt-know-about/. The article was posted on February 27, 2015 by Lindsay Gary.

In Chapter 8, "Our Forefathers of Inventions and Business", the information was taken from Wikipedia entitled "List of African-American Inventors and Scientists" (http://en.wikipedia.org/wiki/List_of_African-American_inventors_and_scientists):

1. Carver, George Washington. 1916. "How to Grow the Peanut and 105 Ways of Preparing it for Human Consumption" (http://aggie-horticulture.tamu.edu/fruit-nut/carver-peanut). Tuskegee Institute Experimental Station Bulletin 31.
2. "Interview with CNBC's "How I Made my Millions" " (http://www.thelifefiles.com/2010/09/22/meet-lonnie-johnson-he-made-millions-selling-water-guns/). Thelifefiles.com Retrieved 2 April 2018.
3. Roche, Timothy. Soaking In Success (http://www.time.com/time/magazine/article/0,9171,998696,00.html). Time magazine. December 4, 2000.
4. Products Created by Independent Inventors (http://www.inventorsdigest.com/?page_id=168) April 2, 2009. Inventors Digest.
5. "Dr. Harold Amos, 84; Mentor to Aspiring Minority Physicians" (http://articles.latimes.com/2003/mar/08/local/me-passings8.2) Los Angeles Times. 2003-03-08. Retrieved 2011-03-11.

6. "George Edward Alcom, Jr" (http://inventors.about.com/library/inventors/blbennett.htm). About.com. Retrieved 2008-02-27.
7. "Alcom excelled in missile research" (http://www.post-gazette.com/lifestyle/20020220kids0220p9.asp) Pittsburgh Post-Gazette. February 20, 2002. Retrieved 2008-02-27. "George Edward Alcom Jr. attended Occidential College in Los Angeles where he earned eight letters in basketball and football and was an honors student studying physics. He received his bachelor's degree in 1962 and a master's in nuclear physics from Howard University a year later.
8. Andrews, J. J.; Curtis, M. L. (1965). "Free groups and handlebodies". Proceedings of the American Mathematical Society, 16 (2): 192 – 195, JSTOR 2033843 (https://www.jstor.org/stable/2033843),
9. [1] (http://www.google.com/patents/USRE11830), "Folding Bed"
10. Mendheim, Beverly (September 2007). "Lost and Found: Alice Augusta Ball, an Extraordinary Woman of Hawai'i Nei" (http://northwesthawaiitimes.com/hnsept07.htm). Northwest Hawaii Times. Retrieved 20 May 2013.
11. The ninth and tenth paragraphs of the "His Story" (http://www.bannekermemorial.org/history.htm) page in official website of the Washington Interdependence Council (http://www.bannekermemorial.org): Administrators of the Benjamin Banneker Memorial (Retrieved 2008-08-06), the fourth paragraph in the webpage entitled "Who was Benjamin Banneker?" (http://benjaminbanneker.k12.dc.us/benjamin_banneker.html) Archived 2012-06-29 at WebCite in official website of the Benjamin Banneker Academic High School (http://benjaminbanneker.k12.dc.us) Archived (https://www.webcitation.org/6ASkjirhJ?url=http://benjaminbanneker.k12.dc.us/) 2012-09-06 at WebCite, 800 Euclid Street, NW, Washington, D.C. 20001 (Retrieved 2009-11-12),

the fourth paragraph in the section entitled "BENJAMIN BANNEKER (1731 – 1806)" in "Benjamin Banneker" page (http://www.nathanielturner.com/benbanneker2.htm) in website of "ChickenBones: A Journal for Literary & Artistic African-American Themes" (http://www.nathanielturner.com) (Retrieved 2008-08-06), the third paragraph in Newbold, K., "Benjamin Banneker: A Brief Biography" (http://www.jmu.edu/madison/center/main_pages/madison_archives/era/african/free/banneker/bio.htm) in official website of The James Madison Center (http://www.jmu.edu/madison/center/home.htm). James Madison University, Harrisonburg, Virginia (Retrieved 2008-10-23), the first paragraph in the webpage entitled "Benjamin Banneker (1731 – 1806)" (http://www.bnl.gov/bera/activities/globe/banneker.htm) in official website of the Brookhaven National Laboratory (http://www.bnl.gov) (Retrieved 2008-08-08), the fifth and sixth paragraphs in "Benjamin Banneker (http://www.blackinventor.com/pages/benjaminbanneker.html) in website of " The Black Inventor Online Museum" (http://www.blackinventor.com) by Adscape International, LLC (Retrieved 2009-0202). An Early American Hero: Benjamin Banneker (http://www.successmaker.com/Subscriver/1,22/ReadingActivities/hero.html#reading) in website of SuccessMaker Enterprise (http://www.successmaker.com) by Pearson Education, Inc. (Retrieved 2009-02-09) and the 1970 book by Claude Lewis entitled Benjamin Banneker; the man who saved Washington, New York, McGraw-Hill, relate part or all of this urban legend.

12. Institute for Advanced Study: A Community of Scholars (http://www.las.edu/people/cos/frontpage?page=8) Archived (https://web.archive.org/web/20130106144422/http://www.ias.edu/poeople/cos/frontpage?page=8) 2013-01-06 at the Wayback Machine.
13. Janet Emerson Bashen (http://inventors.about.com/od/blackinventors/a/bashen.htm), Retrieved from About.com website March 14, 2011.
14. Henderson, Susan K. (1 March 1998), African-American Inventors III. Capstone Press. P. 12. ISBN 978-1-56065-698-2.
15. Johnson Publishing Company (February 4, 2002). "Modern Black Inventors" (https://books.google.com/books?id=AbUDAAAAMBAJ). Jet. Johnson Publishing Company. 101 (7): 55. ISSN 0021-5996 (https://www.worldcat.org/issn/0021-5996). Retrieved 25 February 2011.
16. Lambert, Laura (1 September 2007). Inventors and Inventions. Marshall Cavendish. P. 72. ISBN 978-07614-7763-1.
17. Bellis, Mary (2008). "Andrew Beard (1849 – 1921)" (http://inventors.about.com/library/inventors/blbeard.htm). About.com: Inventors. Retrieved 2008-02-14.
18. Earl S. Bell (http://inventors.about.com/od/blackinventors/a/black_historyB-2.htm). Retrieved from About.com website June 06, 2011.
19. Earl S. Bell (http://appft1.uspto.gov/netacgi/nph-Parser?Sect1=PTO2&Sect2=HITOFF&p=1&u=%2Fnetahtml%2FPTO%2Fsearch-bool.html&r=2&f=G&l=50&co1=AND&d=PG01&s1=%22bell+earl+s%22.IN.&OS=IN/%22bell+earl+s%22&RS=IN/%22bell+earl+s%22). Retrieved from uspto.gov website June 06, 2011.

20. Earl S. Bell (http://atlantapost.com/2011/01/10/contemporary-african-americans-inventors/71). Retrieved from atlantapost.com website June 06, 2011.
21. Bellis, Mary. Inventors: Miriam Benjamin (http://inventors.about.com/library/inventors/blbenjamin.htm). Retrieved from About.com website, February 17, 2011.
22. "Deaths, University of Chicago Magazine, April 96" (http://magazine.uchicago.edu/9604/9604BOBDeaths.html). Magazine.uchicago.edu. Retrieved 2 April 2018.
23. Williams, Scott W. (2008). "Mathematicians of the African Diaspora: Albert Turner Bharucha-Reid" (http://www.math.buffalo.edu/mad/PEEPS/bharucha-reid_a_t.html). The Mathematics Department of the State University of New York at Buffalo. Retrieved 2012-11-25.
24. Keith Black; Arnold Mann (2009-03-25). Brain Surgeon: A Doctor's Inspiring Encounters with Mortality and Miracles. Grand Central Life & Style. ISBN 978-0446-58109-7.
25. Michael D. Lemonick, "The Tumor War" (http://www.time.com/time/reports/heroes/tumor.html). TIME, Heroes of Medicine special edition, Fall 1997 (retrieved May 15, 2009).
26. Cattau, Daniel (July 2009). "David Blackwell 'Superstar'". Illinois Alumni. University of Illinois Alumni Association. pp. 32-34.
27. Maryland's African American Heritage: Henry Blair (http://library.thinkquest.org/3337/blair.html) Archived (https://web.archive.org/web/20110728105254/http://library.thinkquest.org/3337/blair.html) 2011-07-28 at the Wayback Machine., ThinkQuest.
28. "African American Inventors You Should Know: Henry Blair" (http://inventors.about.com/od/blackinventors/a/Henry_Blair.htm). About.com. Retrieved 2 April 2018.
29. Kwabena Boahen, PhD. Associate Professor of bioengineering (http://bioengineering.stanford.edu/faculty/boahen.html)

Archived (https://web.archive.org/web/20100616064723/http://bioengineering.stanford.edu/faculty/boahen.html) 2010-06-16 at the Wayback Machine. Stanford Bioengineering. Stanford School of Medicine. 2013.
30. IBM Seeks to Build the Computer of the Future Based on Insights from the Brain: IBM Awarded DARPA Funding for Cognitive Computing Collaboration (http://www-03.ibm.com/press/us/en/pressrelease/26123.wss). IBM Alden, November 20, 2008.
31. Sarah Boone (http://www.blackinventor.com/pages/sarah-boone.html). The Black Inventor On-Line Museum, Accessed December 6, 2012.
32. "Ironing-board" (https://patents.google.com/patent/US473653A/en). Google.com. Retrieved 2 April 2018.
33. "Sarah Boone, 7th March 1878 ?" (http://historywoman.weebly.com/1/post/2013/03/sarah-boone-7th-march-1878.html) The History Woman. Retrieved 2 April 2018.
34. Terry, Don (July27, 2008), "Insider has Obama's ear. What's she telling him?" (https://web.archive.org/web/20080729102408/http://www.chicagotribune.com/news/politics/chi-072708-jarrett,0,1640738.story) on July 29, 2008. Retrieved 2008-08-23.

35. "The Bowman Society" (https://web.archive.org/web/20080724084205/http://pritzker.bsd.uchicago.edu/about/news/pritzkerpulse/2005spring/bowman.shtml). Pritzker Pulse. Pritzker School of Medicine, University of Chicago. Spring 2005. Archived from the original (http://pritzker.bsd.uchicago.edu/about/news/pritzkerpulse/2005spring/bowman.shtml) on July 24, 2008. Retrieved March 15, 2009.

36. U.S. Department of Energy. Black Contributors to Science and Energy Technology (Biographical sketch: Otis Boykin) (http://www.africanafrican.com/negroartist/writings/BLACK%20CONTRIBUTORS/BLACK%20CONTRIBUTORS_Page_08.jpg). U.S Department of Energy, Office of Public Affairs, U.S. Government Printing Office, Washington, D.C., 1979, pp. 8-9, DOE/OPA-0035(79).
37. Mary Bellis, "Otis Boykin" (http://inventors.about.com/od/bstartinventors/a/Otis_Boykin.htm). About.com Guide.
38. "Inventor of Heart Stimulator Honored At Memorial Service." Dallas Morning News. March 18, 1962. P. 88.
39. University of Illinois biography (http://chemistry.uiuc.edu/bios/brady.html) Archived (https://web.archive.org/web/20060903230903/http://www.chemisty.uiuc.edu/bios/brady.html) 2006-09-03 at the Wayback Machine, University of Illinois.
40. "PNAS Classics – Protein Structure" (http://www.pnas.org/misc/classics1.shtml). Pnas.org. Retrieved 2 April 2018.
41. Einseberg, David (2003). "The discovery of the alpha-helix and beta-sheet, the principal structural features of proteins: (https://www.ncbi.nlm.nih.gov/pmc/articles/PMC208735) PNAS. 100 (20). 11207 – 11210. Doi: 10.1073/pnas.2034522100 (https://doi.org/10.1073%2Fpnas.2034522100). PMC 208735 (https://www.ncbi.nlm.nih.gov/pmc/articles/PMC208735) PMID 12966187 (https://www.ncbi.nlm.nih.gov/pubmed/12966187).
42. "Henry Brown" (http://www.blackinventor.com/pages/henrybrown). Blackinventor.com. Retrieved 2010-02-06.
43. "The History of Horseshoes" (http://inventors.about.com/library/inventors/blhorseshoe.htm). Inventors – About.com. Retrieved 2015-02-26.

44. Bellis, Mary. "John Albert Burr" (http://inventors.about.com/library/inventors/bl_John_Albert_Burr.htm). About.com. Retrieved 2013-07-22.
45. "Benjamin S. Carson Biography (1951-)" (http://www.faqs.org/health/bios/63/Benjamin-S-Carson.html). www.faqs.org. Retrieved 2 April 2018.
46. "Black Leonardo Book" (http://www.time.com/time/magazine/article/0,9171,801330,00.html). Time Magazine. 1941-11-24. Retrieved 2008-08-10.
47. Harlan, Volume 5, p. 481.
48. Special History Study (http://www.nps.gov/applications/parks/gwca/ppdocuments/Special%20History%20Study.pdf) from the National Park Service website.
49. The legacy of George Washington Carver-Friends & Colleagues (Henry Wallace) (http://www.lib.iastate.edu/spcl/gwc/friends/friends8.html) Archived (https://web.archive.org/web/20090415211140/http://www.lib.iastate.edu/spcl/gwc/friends/friends8.htm) 2009-04-15 at the Wayback Machine.
50. "A Successful Negro Aviator. Charles Ward Chappelle Invents and Aeroplane Which Attacks Attention." News/Opinion, Savannah Tribune, Page 1, February 11, 1911. Savannah, Georgia.
51. "Mr. C.W. Chappelle: The Man, His Life, His Work And His Aspirations." The Gold Coast Nation. Page 3. June 28, 1919. Ghana.
52. The Crises: A Record of the Darker Races, "Social Uplift" (page 7), published by the National Association of Colored People (NAACP), May 11, 1911 in New York City.
53. Bio. True Story, "Kenneth Bancroft Clark Biography." Accessed December 7, 2012. http://www.biography.com/people/kenneth-bancroft-clark-9249475

54. McCoy, Frank (1999-12-26). "He refined the desktop PC. Now he wants to kill it" (https://web.archive.org/web/20121020094411/http://www.usnews.com/usnews/culture/articles/000103/archive_034033.htm).
U.S. News & World Report. Archived from the original (https://www.usnews.com/usnews/culture/articles/000103/archive_034033.htm) on 2012-10-20. Retrieved 2011-08-12. "A year later, Dean led a team that built a 1,000-megahertz chip [...]"
55. Angel, Jonathan (2011-08-10). "Thirty years later, the personal computer's obsolete, IBM PC designer says" (https://archive.is/20120904035652/http://www.linuxfordevices.com/c/a/News/IBM-PC-thirtieth-anniversary/). Linixfordevices.com. Archived from the original (http://www.linuxfordevices.com/c/a/News/IBM-PC-thirtieth-anniversary/) on 2012-09-04. Retrieved 2011-08-12.
56. Dean, Mark (2011-08-12). "IBM Leads the Way in the Post-PC Era" (http://asmarterplanet.com/blog/2011/08/ibm-leads-the-way-in-the-post-pc-era.html). A Smarter Planet. Retrieved 2011-08-12. "I recently traded in my PC for a tablet computer [...]"
57. "ANNIE JEAN EASLEY's Obituary on The Plain Dealer" (http://obits.cleveland.com/obituaries/cleveland/obituary.aspx?n=annie-jean-easley&pid=152269470). The Plain Dealer. Retrieved 2 April 2018.
58. "ANNIE JEAN EASLEY's Obituary on The Plain Dealer" (http://obits.cleveland.com/obituaries/cleveland/obituary.aspx?n=annie-jean-easley&pid=152269470). The Plain Dealer. Retrieved 2 April 2018.
59. "Interview code OHI0026830" (http://www.jsc.nasa.gov/history/oral_histories/NASA_HQ/Herstory/EasleyAJ/AJE_8-21-01.pdf) (PDF). Nasa.gov. Retrieved 2 April 2018.

60. Skip Ellis (http://www.math.buffalo.edu/mad/computer-science/ellis_clarencea.html). Retrieved from Computer Scientists of the African Diaspora web site March 6, 2012.
61. Skip Ellis (http://express.howstuffworks.com/ep-ellis.htm). Retrieved from howstuffworks Extraordinary People website, March 6, 2012.
62. "Lloyd Ferguson, a pioneering African American professor/chemist from Cal State L.A., has died" (https://web.archive.org/web/20150924035237/http://www.insightnews.com/news/8333-lloyd-ferguson-apioneering-african-american-professorchemist-from-cal-state-la-has-died). Insight News. December 28, 2011, archived from the original (http://www.insightnews.com/news/8333-lloyd-ferguson-a-pioneering-african-american-professorchemist-from-cal-state-la-has-died) on September 24, 2015
63. "Biographical Snapshots of Famous Women and Minority Chemists" (http://jchemed.chem.wisc.edu/JCEWWW/Features/eChemists/Bios/Ferguson.html). Journal of Chemical Education. Retrieved 2011-01-17. Contribution=ignored (help).
64. Kessler, J.H.; Kidd, J.S.; Kidd, R. A.; Morin, K.H. (1996), Distinguished African American Scientists of the 20th Century, Phoenix, AZ: Oryx Press, pp. 94-99, ISBN 978-0-89774-955-8
65. "UMD PCAST announcement" (http://www.newsdesk.umd.edu/scitech/print.cfm?articleID=1882) University of Maryland. Retrieved 2009-04-30.
66. Gates, S. James; M.T. Grisaru; M. Rocek; W. Siegel (1983). "Superspace" (https://arxiv.org/find/hep-th/1/AND+au:+gates+ti:+lesson/0/1/0/all/0/1). American Institute of Physics.
67. "Sarah Goode" (http://www.blackinventor.com/pages/sarah-goode.html). Inventors. The Black Inventor On-Line Museum. 2011. Retrieved 13 November 2011.
68. "Sarah E. Goode" (http://www.csupomona.edu/~plin/inventors/goode.html). Inventors. Retrieved 13 November 2011.

69. Vrable, Jim (2004). When in Boston: A Time Line & Almanac. Northeastern University Press. P. 238. ISBN 9781555536213.
70. Dr. Joseph L. Graves, Jr. (http://www.wolfmanproductions.com/graves.html) Archived (https://web.archive.org/web/20120206120027/http://www.wolfmanproductions.com/graves.html) 2012-02-06 at the Wayback Machine.
71. Graves, Joseph L. (January 1, 2002). "The Biological Case Against Race" (https://web.archive.org/web/20061115040049/http://www.heartland.org/pdf/12721n.pdf) (PDF). American Outlook. Archived from the original (http://www.heartland.org/pdf/12721n.pdf) (PDF) on November 15, 2006. Retrieved November 15, 2006.
72. Joseph L. Graves, Jr., Ph.D. (http://www.minority.unc.edu/institute/2006/spkrbios/JosephGraves.cfm) Archived (https://web.archive.org/web/20070622203700/http://www.minority.unc.edu/institute/2006/spkrbios/JosephGraves.cfm) 2007-06-22 at the Wayback Machine.
73. "Alumni Honored at Black Engineer Gala News and Current Events, A. James Clark School of Engineering, University of Maryland" (http://www.engr.umd.edu/news/news_story.php?id=258). Engr.umd.edu. 2006-02-20. Retrieved 2009-03-28.
74. "Bessie Blount Griffin" (https://web.archive.org/web/20090301140918/http://www.csupomona.edu/~plin/inventors/blount.html). www.csupomona.edu. Archived from the original (http://www.csupomona.edu/~plin/inventors/blount.html) on 2009-03-01. Retrieved 2010-01-05.
75. "Virginia Women in History Past Honorees" (http://www.lva.virginia.gov/public/vawomen/2006/pasthonorees.htm). www.lva.virginia.gov. Retrieved 2010-01-05.

76. "James A. Harris" (http://jchemed.chem.wisc.edu/JCEWWW/features/echemists/Bios/Harris.html). Journal of Chemical Education. Retrieved 27 May 2011.
77. McMurray, Emily, ed. Notable Twentieth-Century Scientists. Gale Research, Inc.: Detroit, 1995.
78. Singing In The Brain (http://www.dukemagazine.duke.edu/dukemag/issues/070802/depupd.html) Archived (https://web.archive.org/web/20081007063444/http://www.dukemagazine.duke.edu/dukemag/issues/070802/depupd.html) 2008-10-07 at the Wayback Machine. , Duke Magazine, November-December 2001.
79. Duke News (http://www.dukemednews.duke.edu/news/article.php?id=9272) Archived (https://web.archive.org/web/20070609215129/http://www.dukemednews.duke.edu/news/article.php?id=9272) 2007-06-09 at the Wayback Machine.
80. Erich Jarvis Named Howard Hughes Investigator (http://www.dukehealth.org/HealthLibrary/News/10333 Archived (https://web.archive.org/web/20080921214308/http://www.dukehealth.org/HealthLibrary/News/10333) 2008-09-21 at the Wayback Machine., Duke Medicine News & Communications. Retrieved from Dukehealth.org.
81. Bicycle Frame, Patent number: 634823, Filing date: April 6, 1898, Issue date: October 10, 1899 (http://www.google.com/patents/US634823?printsec=description#v=onepage), United States Patent Office.
82. Soaking in Success (http://www.time.com/time/magazine/article/0,9171,998696,00.html), By Timothy Roche. December 4, 2000. TIME.

83. Shooting for the Sun (https://www.theatlantic.com/magazine/archive/2010/11/shooting-for-the-sun/8268/1/), By Logan Ward, October 2010. The Atlantic
84. Lonni Johnson – Thermo-Electric Generator – articles, patent (http://www.rexresearch.com/johnsonjtec/johnson-th.htm), The Rex Research Civilization Kit.
85. Rebecca Goodman: Barrett J. Brunsman (2005-02-28). This Day In Ohio History (https://books.google.com/books?id=3IJtVP9WnXEC&pg=PA214) Emmis Books. P. 214 ISBN 978-1-57860-191-2.
86. "A Science Odyssey: People and Discoveries: Percy Julian" (https://www.pbs.org/wgbh/aso/databank/entries/bmjuli.html). www.pbs.org. Retrieved 2 April 2018.
87. "Percy Lavon Julian" (https://www.sciencehistory.org/historical-profile/percy-lavon-julian). Science History Institute. Retrieved 21 March 2018.
88. "Giants of the Past: Percy Lavon Julian (1899 – 1975) A Forgotten Pioneer in Soy" (http://www.ars.usda.gov/research/publications/publications.htm?seq_no_115=215771). United States Department of Agriculture. Retrieved February 18, 2012.
89. "Percy Lavon Julian (1899 – 1975)" (https://web.archive.org/web/20120415001340/http://lipidlibrary.aocs.org/history/Julian/index.htm). Lipid Library. Archived from the original (http://lipidlibrary.aocs.org/history/Julian/index.htm) on April 15, 2012. Retrieved February 18, 2012.
90. Kelsey, Elizabeth. "Expansive Vision, Ahead of His Time: Dartmouth celebrates biologist E. E. Just, Class of 1907" (http://www.dartmouth.edu/~dartlife/archives/18-6/just.html). Dartmouth Life. Dartmouth College. Retrieved 2009-01-28.

91. Manning, Kenneth R. (1984). Black Apollo of science: the life of Ernest Everett Just. New York: Oxford University Press. ISBN 978-0195034981.
92. Lee, Edward (March 2006). "Ernest Everett Just". Blacfax: 15-16.
93. Allen, Arthur (12 May 200). "Flesh and blood and DNA" (http://www.salon.com/health/feature/2000/05/12/roots/index.html). Salon. Retrieved 13 May 2011.
94. "African American Lives 2, PBS" (https://www.pbs.org/wnet/aalives/science_dna2.html). Pbs.org. Retrieved 2 April 2018.
95. "Samuel L. Kountz Diversity Fellowship – General Surgery – Stanford Medicine" (http://med.stanford.edu/gensurg/education/kountz.html). Med.stanford.edu. Retrieved 2 April 2018.
96. Organ, CH Jr. "The black surgeon in the twentieth century: a tribute to Samuel L. Kountz, MD" (https://www.ncbi.nlm.nih.gov/pmc/articles/PMC2537148). J Natl Med Assoc. 70: 683 – 4. PMC 2537148 (https://www.ncbi.nlm.nih.gov/pmc/articles/PMC2537148) PMID 359824 (https://www.ncbi.nlm.nih.gov/pubmed/359824).
97. – Encyclopedia of Arkansas (http://www.encyclopediaofarkansas.net/encyclopedia/entry-detail.aspx?entryID=18)
98. Altman, Lawrence K. "DR. SAMUEL KOUNTZ, 51 DIES; LEADER IN TRANSPLANT SURGERY" (https://www.nytimes.com/1981/12/24/obituaries/dr-samuel-kountz-51-dies-leader-in-transplant-surgery.html). Nytimes.com. Retrieved 2 April 2018.
99. Rayvon Fouche (2003). Black inventors in the Age of Segregation: Granville T. Woods, Lewis H. Latimer, & Shelby J. Davidson. JHU Press. ISBN 978-0-8018-7319-5.
100. Clark, John Henrik (1983), Ivan Van Sertima, ed. Blacks in Science: Ancient and Modern. Piscataway, NJ: Transaction. Pp. 230-233. ISBN 978-0-87855-941-1.

101. "Lewis Howard Latimer" (http://www.nps.gov/edis/forkids/the-gifted-men-who-worked-for-edison.htm). National Park Service. Retrieved 2007-06-10.
102. List of 2006 NIHF inductees (http://www.invent.org/2006Induction/historical2006.asp) Archived (https://web.archive.org/web/20080513143652/http://www.invent.org/2006Induction/historical2006.asp) 2008-05-13 at the Wayback Machine.
103. "Fairchild Channel F – The First ROM Cartridge Console" (http://classicgames.about.com/od/classicvideogames101/p/FairchildChannelFProfile.htm). About.com.
104. Weber, Bruce (April 13, 2011). "Gerald A. Lawson, Video Game Pioneer, Dies at 70" (https://www.nytimes.com/2011/04/13/technology/personaltech/14lawson.html). The New York Times.
105. Mahoney, Mary. "Mary Eliza" (https://www.pbs.org/wgbh/amex/partners/early/e_pioneers_mahoney.html). American Experience. PBS.
106. "Jan Matzeliger" (http://www.blackinventor.com/pages/jan-matzeliger.html). The Black Inventor Online Museum.
107. "Inventor of the Week / Jan Matzeliger" (http://web.mit.edu/invent/iow/matzeliger.html). Massachusetts Institute of Technology. August 2002.
108. Brown, Mitchell, [www.lib.lsu.edu/lib/chem/display/henry-mcbay.html "Faces of Science: African-Americans in the Sciences,"] 1996.
109. Kessler, James H., J.S. Kidd, Renee A. Kidd, and Katherine A. Morin. Distinguished African-American Scientists of the 20th Century. Oryx Press: Phoenix, AZ, 1996.
110. "The not-so-real McCoy" (https://web.archive.org/web/20110517111621/http://www33.brinkster.com/iiiii/mccoy/). Archived from the original (http://www33.brinkster.com/iiiii/mccoy/) on 2011-05-17.

111. "Elijah McCoy, Inventor of the Week" (http://web.mit.edu/invent/iow/mccoy.html). Lemelson MIT Program. May 1996. Retrieved August 18, 2011.
112. Article outlining McLurkin's "Innovative Lives" presentation for the Smithsonian's Lemelson Center (http://invention.smithsonian.org/centerpieces/ilives/lecture02.html) Archived (https://web.archive.org/web/20080704052509/http://invention.smithsonian.org/centerpieces/ilives/lecture02.html) 2008-07-04 at the Wayback Machine.
113. "Willie Hobbs Moore, first African American Woman Physicist" (http://www.math.buffalo.edu/mad/physics/moore_williehobbs.html). www.math.buffalo.edu. Retrieved 2 April 2018.
114. Tough, Paul (12 December 2004). "'Acting white' Myth, The" (https://www.nytimes.com/2004/12/12/magazine/acting-white-myth-the.html). Retrieved 2 April 2018 – via NYTimes.com.
115. "Acting White manuscript" (http://www.economics.harvard.edu/faculty/fryer/files/Empiriccal%2Banalysis%2Bof%2B%2527acting%2Bwhite%2527_final%2Bmanuscript.pdg) (PDF). Harvard.edu. Retrieved 2 April 2018.
116. Bike, William S. "Essays on Earl Renfroe" [2] (https://www.amazon.com/Essays-Earl-Renfroe-Man-Firsts/dp/0971045909). UIC College of Dentistry Press, 2001.
117. Janega, James. Chicago Tribune. "Dr. Earl Renfroe Sr., 93, Pioneering Orthodontist." [3] (http://articles.chicagotribune.com/2000-11-23/news/0011230214_1_orthodontics-african-american-dental).
118. Norbert Rillieux, invention of the multiple-effect evaporator (http://www.inventions-license.com/view_inventor.php?id=89). Inventions-license.com Accessed December 4, 2012.

119. Bellis, Mary. "Walter Sammons" (http://inventors.about.com/library/inventors/bl_Walter_Sammons.htm). Retrieved 27 May 2011.
120. "Townhall.com" (http://www.townhall.com/columnists/thomassowell/ts20030108.shtml). Townhall.com. Retrieved 2010-04-06.
121. "Townhall.com" (http://www.townhall.com/columnists/thomassowell/ts20030109.shtml). Townhall.com. Retrieved 2010-04-06.
122. Larry D. Nachman, "A Conflict of Visions, by Thomas Sowell" (http://www.commentarymagazine.com/article/a-conflict-of-visions-by-thomas-sowell/). Commentary, March 1987.
123. "Thomas Sowell" (http://jewishworldreview.com/cols/sowell010036.php3). Jewishworldreview.com. Retrieved 2010-03-12.
124. NCTM past presidents (http://www.nctm.org/about/content.aspx?id=852). Retrieved 2011-03-20.
125. Lewis Temple (http://www.blackinventor.com/pages/lewis-temple.html). Black Inventor Online Museum. Accessed December 6, 2012.
126. (1985) Pioneering Research in Surgical Shock and Cardiovascular Surgery: Vivien Thomas and His Work with Alfred Blalock, University of Pennsylvania Press, pp. 9-13. ISBN 0-8122-7989-1.
127. "Almost a Miracle" (https://web.archive.org/web/20120302102051/http://www.hopkinsmedicine.org/dome/0301/close-up.cfm). Hopkinsmedicine.org. Archived from the original (http://www.hopkinsmedicine.org/dome/0301/close_up.cfm) on 2012-03-02. Retrieved 2012-03-08.
128. OAH Award Winners (http://www.oah.org/activities/awards/barnouw/winners.html)

Archived (https://web.archive.org/web/20090603010229/http://www.oah.org/activities/awards/barnouw/winners.html) 2009-06-03 at the Wayback Machine., OAH Erik Barncuw Award Winners.
129. "Abramson, Charles I. (2009). "A study in inspiration: Charles Henry Turner (1867 – 1923) and the investigation of insect behavior". Annual Review of Entomology. ISSN 0066-4170 (https://www.worldcat.org/issn/0066-4170) PMID 18817509 (https://www.ncbi.nlm.nih.gov/pubmed/18817509).
130. Branch, Danny Heise, Scientific Information Technology. "Directory of phone and e-mail for all staff" (https://www.niams.nih.gov/About_Us/Phone_Directory/individual_page.asp). www.niams.nih.gov. Retrieved 2017-02-09.
131. "Symposium Awards" (http://www.nationalspacesymposium.org/about/awards/douglas-s-morrow-public-outreach-award). National Space Symposium. Retrieved October 25, 2010.
132. "Neil deGrasse Tyson" (https://web.archive.org/web/20130320231400/http://www.thegreatcourses.com/tgc/professors/professor_detail.aspx?pid=257). The Great Courses. Archived from the original http://www.thegreatcourses.com/tgc/professors/professor_detail.aspx?pid=257) on March 20, 2013. Retrieved June 13, 2012.
133. Blum, Matt (August 5, 2011). "Cosmos Will Get a Sequel Hosted by Neil deGrasse Tyson" (https://www.wired.com/geekdad/2011/08/cosmos-to-get-a-sequel-hosted-by-neil-degrasse-tyson/). Wired. Retrieved August 5, 2011.
134. James Glanz, Arthur Walker, 64, Scientist and Mentor, Dies (https://www.nytimes.com/2001/05/09/us/arthur-walker-64-scientist-and-mentor-dies.html). The New York Times (May 9, 2001).
135. Dawn Levy, Art Walker: 'favorite sun' of solar physics (http://news.stanford.edu/news/2000/october4/walkerprofile-104.html). Stanford Report (October 4, 2000).

136. Dawn Levy. Solar physicist Art Walker dies at 64; pioneer in X-ray optics (http://news.stanford.edu/news/2001/may2/walkerobit-52.html). Stanford Report (May 2, 2001).
137. NCAR's Warren Washington elected chair of National Science Board (http://www.cisl.ucar.edu/news/02/features/0510.washington.html) May 10, 2002.
138. Warren M. Washington Collection (http://www.ucar.edu/library/collections/washington/). National Center for Atmospheric Research.
139. Warren Washington Receives National Science Medal (http://www2.ucar.edu/news/2890/warren-washington-receives-national-medal-science). National Center for Atmospheric Research. University Corporation for Atmospheric Research, October 15, 2010.
140. Warren M. Washington: Senior Scientist & Head of the Climate Change Research Section, Climate and Global Dynamics Division, The National Center for Atmospheric Research (http://sites.nationalacademies.org/PGA/cwsem/PGA_045077). National Academy of Sciences.
141. "James B. West of WSE receives Benjamin Franklin Medal: Johns Hopkins University – The Gazette" (http://gazette.jhu.edu/2010/05/10/james-b-west-of-wse-receives-benjamin-franklin-medal/). Gazette.jhu.edu. 2010-05-10. Retrieved 2010-03-09.
142. "Ian Moss: America's Diversity Can Provide Prosperity" (http://www.huggingtonpost.com/ian-moss/americas-diversity-can-pr_b_469787.html). Huffingtonpost.com. Retrieved 2012-03-09.
143. "Invent Now |Hall of Fame | Search | Inventor Profile" (https://web.archive.org/web/20120215021322/http://www.invent.org/hall_of_fame/150.html). Invent.org. 1931-02-10. Archived from the original (http://www.invent.org/hall_of_fame/150.html) on 2012-02-15. Retrieved 2012-03-09.

144. "Services Update" (http://www.ieee.org/web/aboutus/history_center/biography/wilkins.html). www.ieee.org. Retrieved 2 April 2018.
145. "University of Chicago to commemorate accomplishments of mathematics alumnus J. Ernest Wilkins Jr." (http://www-news.uchicago.edu/releases/07/070227.wilkins.shtml). www-news.uchicago.edu. Retrieved 2 April 2018.
146. Zerbonia, Ralph G. (contrib. by Alic, Margaret) (2005) Contemporary Black Biography (https://books.google.com/books?ei=5LfxSezpMZHGzASv0KyVCw). Gale Research Inc, 2005, Vol. 49 (Original from the University of Michigan). Digitized Sep. 17, 2008, ISBN 0-7876-6731-5, ISBN 978-0-7876-6731-3. (biography viewable via Answers.com (http://www.answers.com/top/j-ernest-wilins-jr)).
147. Daniel Hale Williams#cite note-Schumacker-3
148. Cato Editors (2011-03-31). "Happy Birthday Walter Williams" (http://www.cato-at-liberty.org/happy-birthday-walter-williams/). Cato@Liberty.
149. Williams, Walter (August 25, 1997). "Capitalism and the Common Man" (http://www.fee.org/the_freeman/detail/capitalism-and-the-common-man). Retrieved March 20, 2013.
150. Williams, Walter. "The Pursuit of Happiness – Economics for the Citizen" (http://www.thefreemanonline.org/columns/the-pursuit-of-happiness-economics-for-the-citizen/). The Freeman. Retrieved December 6, 2010.
151. Bellis, Mary. Granville T. Woods, 1856 – 1910 (http://invetors.about.com/od/wstartinventors/a/GranvilleTWoods.htm).
152. Kwame Anthony Appiah, Henry Louis Gates – Africana: Civil Rights: An A-to-Z Reference of the Movement that Changed America (https://books.google.com/books?id=EFgB5O1OMrMC&pg=PA464)

153. "Kenyon College" (http://northbysouth.kenyon.edu/1998/health/wright.htm) Northbysouth.kenyon.edu. Retrieved 2012-02-01.
154. Monday, Oct. 29, 1934 (1934-10-29) "Medicine: Negro Fellow> Time Magazine, 29th October 1934" (http://www.time.com/time/magazine/article/0,9171,882266,00.html). Time.com. Retrieved 2012-02-01.
155. Merry Maisel & Laura Smart (1997). "Lifelong Struggle of a Zoologist". Women in Science: A selection of sixteen significant contributors (http://www.sdsc.edu/ScienceWomen/young.hml). The San Diego Supercomputer Center.
156. Young, R.A. (1924). "On the Excretory Apparatus in Paramecium", Science. 60 (1550): 244. Doi: 10.1126/Science.60.1550.244 (https://doi.org/10.1126%2Fscience.60.1550.244) JSTOR 1649643 (https://www.jstor.org/stable/1649643). PMID 17814573 (https://www.ncbi.nlm.nih.gov/pubmed/17814573).

In Chapter 8, "Our Forefathers of Inventions and Business", the information about Dr. Shirley Jackson, Lewis Latimer, Marie Van Brittan Brown, Otis Boykin, Lonnie G. Johnson, Charles Drew, Marian R. Croak, Lisa Gelobter, Phillip Emeagwali, Jesse Earnest Wilkins, Jr., Elijah McCoy, Garrett Morgan, and Mary and Mildred Davidson was taken from the article entitled "14 Black Inventors You Probably Didn't Know About by: Pamela Rosario Perez (Feb. 26, 2017) http://thinkgrowth.org/14-black-inventors-you-probably-didnt-know-about-3c0702cc63d2.

In Chapter 9, "Diane Thomas-Newbill...the Author", the information about Classic Lawncare & Building Maintenance is found at two websites: http://www.clbm.net (The social/mission side) and http://www.classiclawncarebuildingmaintenance.com (business information).

Diane has currently written **9 books that are found on Amazon.com.** See the information below for more information about her books:

1. **The Man Across the Street**: ISBN-13: 978-1492280729, **Paperback**, 144 pages. Fiction/Fairytales/Folk-tales, Legend & Mythology. Publication date: May 2, 2015.
   Kindle eBook: ASIN: B00X2XWAKA.

2. **On The Playground**: ISBN-13: 978-1514673300, **Paperback**, 24 pages. Family & Relationships/Bullying/ children's book. Publication date: June 30, 2015.
   Kindle eBook: ASIN: B01OOSJLSY.

3. **Painted Lady**: ISBN-13: 978-1518680342, **Paperback**, 26 pages. Book 1 of 6 entitled, "The Family". Family & Relationships/religion/inspirational/child – adult. Publication: October 18, 2015. **Kindle eBook**: ASIN: B0171T8TX2.

4. **Valiant Man**: ISBN-13: 978-1518836206, **Paperback**, 30 pages. Book 2 of 6 entitled, "The Family". Family & Relationships/religion/inspirational/child-adult. Publication: October 29, 2015. **Kindle eBook**: ASIN: B017DXA73G.

5. **A Passionate Life**: ISBN-13: 978-1519587589, **Paperback**, 28 pages. Book 3 of 6 entitled, "The Family". Family & Relationships/religion/inspirational/child-adult. Publication: November 28, 2015. **Kindle eBook**: ASIN: B018PNHEHU.

6. **Leading and Loving You**: ISBN-13: 978-1519659675, **Paperback**, 26 pages. Book 4 of 6 entitled, "The Family". Family & Relationships/religion/inspirational/child-adult. Publication: December 2, 2015. **Kindle eBook**: ASIN: B018YNW4XK.

7. **My Sister Adah**: ISBN-13: 978-1522964995, **Paperback**, 24 pages. Book 5 of 6 entitled, "The Family". Family & Relationships/religion/inspirational/child-adult. Publication: December 28, 2015. **Kindle eBook**: B019YBK9HY.

8. **My Brother Asher**: ISBN-13: 978-1523206490, **Paperback**, 26 pages. Book 6 of 6 entitled, "The Family". Family & Relationships/religion/inspirational/child-adult. Publication: December 31, 2015. **Kindle eBook**: B01A2DS1IW.

9. **The Black Angel**: ISBN-13: 978-1548088781, **Paperback**, 270 pages. Fiction/Fairytales/Folk-tales/Legends & Mythology/religion. Publication: June 13, 2017. **Kindle eBook**: B072NBF6LL.

Appendix B. – Resources:

In this section of the appendix, I want to share different types of resources that I hope will "inspire you" to start your own Black Business. Keep in mind that "inspiring you" is the goal of this book.

In the resources listed below, you will discover books and other information that will help you understand YOUR Black entrepreneurial history and journey. I would encourage you to not only read the list of resources, but to obtain some of the resources for your own knowledge (history and business).

The following information is taken from the Library of Congress, Washington, DC (http://www.loc.gov/rr/business/black) **African American Business Resources:**

The following lists selected Internet resources of particular interest to African Americans in business, including those offered by professional associations, and government agency and trade publishers. Compiled by Angela Wilson and Gail Austin, Business Reference Services, Science, Technology, and Business Division (Library of Congress):

Entrepreneurial Web Resources

- **Black Enterprise**
  http://www.blackenterprise.com (Registration required to access some feature of the site) 130 Fifth Avenue, 10th Floor, New York, NY 10011 *Contains business news, "Business Enterprise 100 Lists, "free downloads, and information on investing and franchising.

- **Minority Business Development Agency**
  http://www.mbda.gov, 14th Street & Constitution Avenue NW, Room 5055, Washington, DC 20230 *Provides access to sources of financing, market opportunities and preparation of financial and bonding proposals.

- **Minority Business Entrepreneur**
  http://www.mbemag.com *Online bimonthly magazine which features a business resources directory and searchable archive of earlier topics.

- **National Black Chamber of Commerce**
  http://www.nationalbcc.org, 1350 Connecticut Avenue, Suite 825, Washington, DC 20036. * Represents 64,000 Black owned businesses with 190 chapters through out the US, Ghana, Bahamas, and Jamaica. **You can also find a local Chamber of Commerce near you.**

- **SCORE** (Service Corps of Retired Executives)
  http://www.score.org, 409 3rd St. SW, 6th Floor, Washington, DC 20024 *Provides free of charge counseling and mentoring from working and retired business owners. **You can also find a SCORE division in a location near you.**

- **Small Business Administration**
  http://www.sba.gov, 1110 Vermont Avenue NW, 9th Floor, Washington, DC 20201 *Offers downloadable publications and workshops on startups, franchising and financing. **You can also find a local SBA servicing center in your area.**

- **Target Market News**
  http://www.targetmarketnews.com, 228 S. Wabash Avenue, Suite 210, Chicago, Illinois 60604 *Provides statistics on the 490 billion dollar black consumer market and includes industry events calendar and career opportunities.

The following list of books, journals, and websites was prepared by: Angela Wilson and Gail Austin, Business References Services. Science, Technology, and Business Division (Library of Congress):

Celebrating African American Business Leaders: Past, Present and Future

Books:

- **African Americans in business: the path towards empowerment: essays on black entrepreneurship from the African background to the present: 73rd national celebration of Afro-American history** / Larry L. Martin, editor-in-chief...[et al.]. Washington, D.C.: Association for the Study of Afro-American Life and History, Inc., c1998. 2 v.: ill.; 28 cm. LC (Library of Congress) Call Number: HD2344.5.U6A37 1998, LC (Library of Congress) Control Number: 99209689.

    This two-volume set contains essays and a learning resource package of Black entrepreneurship from slavery to present day. Volume one contains essays that highlight topics such as Black business activities, leadership, women, corporate America, and future prospects. Access is by table of contents and chapter headings. Volume two is a learning resource package designed to supplement volume one. Part one of volume two contains suggested learning activities and classroom activities accessible by subject sections. Part two of volume two contains teaching strategies and lessons for elementary through secondary levels.

- **Making money the old-fashioned way: a story of Black entrepreneurship** / by Aaron Bocage and George Waters. Camden, NJ (313 Market St., Camden 08102): EDTEC, Inc., c1997. 110 p. :ill. (some col.), map; 28 cm. LC (Library of Congress) Call Number: HD2344.5.U6B63 1997, LC (Library of Congress) Control Number: 98136278.

    This volume offers a historical overview of Black entrepreneurs in the United States. It relates the influence of slavery upon the history of Black entrepreneurship, lists important dates in Black business history, and provides information on contemporary Black entrepreneurs and top business firms. Access is by subject. Separate indexes are provided for information on Black youth entrepreneurship and national Black business related organizations in support of entrepreneurship.

- **Black corporate executives: the making and breaking of a black middle class** / by Sharon M. Collins (1947 -). Philadelphia: Temple University Press, 1997. xv, 198 p.; 22 cm. ISBN 1-56639-473-2 (cloth; alk. paper), ISBN 1-56639-474-0 (pbk.: alk. paper), Series: Labor and Social Change. LC (Library of Congress) Call Number: HD38.25.U6C65 1997, LC (Library of Congress) Control Number: 96010735

- **Black enterprise titans of the B.E. 100s: black CEOs who redefined and conquered American business** / Derek T. Dingle. New York: J. Wiley, c1999. xvi, 238 p.: ill. ; 24 cm. ISBN 0-471-31853-1 (cloth: alk. paper) LC (Library of Congress) Call Number: HD38.25.U6D56 1999, LC (Library of Congress) Control Number: 98051031

- **Economic census. Survey of minority-owned business enterprises.** Washington, D.C.: U.S. Dept. of Commerce,

Bureau of the Census: For sale by Supt. Of Docs., U.S. G.P.O., LC (Library of Congress) Call Number (1992 edition): HD2346.U5E269 1996, LC (Library of Congress) Control Number (1992 edition): 96141790. LC (Library of Congress) Call Number (1997 edition): HD2346.U5E269 2001, LC (Library of Congress) Control Number (1997 edition): 2001330031

Comprehensive survey data on minority businesses. First introduced as special project in 1969 and incorporated into the 1972 Economic Census. Prior to this time, such data on Black business owners was basically nonexistent. Currently called Survey of Business Owners it "provides the only source of detailed and comprehensive data on the status, nature, and scope of women-, minority-, and veteran-owned businesses."

- **Encyclopedia of African American business history** / edited by Juliet E.K. Walker. Westport, Conn.: Greenwood Press, 1999. xxxi, 721 p. ; 24 cm. ISBN 0-313-29549- (acid-free paper) LC (Library of Congress) Call Number: HD2344.5.U6E53 1999, LC (Library of Congress) Control Number: 98044218

- **My soul is my own: oral narratives of African American women in the professions** / Gwendolyn Etter-Lewis. New York: Routledge, 1993. xvii, 213 p. ; 24 cm. ISBN 0-415-90559-1 (hard: acid-free paper), ISBN 0-415-90560-5 (pbk.: acid-free paper). LC (Library of Congress) Call Number: HD6054.4.U6E88 1993, LC (Library of Congress) Control Number: 92039044

- **How to succeed in business without being white: straight talk on making it in America** / Earl G. Graves (1935 -). New York: HarperBusiness, c1997. xviii, 295 p., [8] p. of plates : ill. ; 24 cm. ISBN 0-88730-808-2, LC (Library of Congress) Call Number: HF5386.G675 1997, LC (Library of Congress) Control Number: 96052510

- **African American entrepreneurs** / Jim Haskins (1941). New York: J. Wiley & sons, c1998. (Black stars) viii, 184 p.: ill. ; 25 cm. ISBN 0-471-14576-9 (cloth: alk. paper) LC (Library of Congress) Call Number: HC102.5.A2H37 1998, LC (Library of Congress) Control Number: 97037389

Profiles a variety of African American entrepreneurs, from the early years, through out the Civil War and Reconstruction, to modern times.

- **History of black business: the coming of America's largest black-owned businesses** / by Martin K. Hunt and Jacqueline E. Hunt. Chicago, Ill.: Knowledge Express Co. c1998. 270 p.: ill. ; 24 cm. ISBN 0-9665221-0-9. LC (Library of Congress) Call Number: HD2344.5.U6H86 1998, LC (Library of Congress) Control Number: 99094225

- **African-American business leaders: a biographical dictionary** / John N. Ingham and Lynne B. Feldman. Westport, Conn.: Greenwood Press, c1994. xiv, 806 p.; 25 cm. ISBN 0-313-27253-0 (alk. paper). LC (Library of Congress) Call Number: HC102.5.A2152 1994, LC (Library of Congress) Control Number: 93020430

This collection contains the comprehensive biographies of 123 African American business leaders in seventy-seven separate biographical entries. Focus is placed on the most historically significant Black business leaders from America's early period to present day. Each biography highlights the relevant cultural, economic, and social issues faced by each leader. Access is by alphabetical order and index. Also provided are appendixes listing place of birth, principle place of business, type of business, and women business leaders. A bibliographic essay is also provided.

- **Biographical dictionary of African Americans** / Rachel Kranz and Phillip J. Koslow. New York: Facts on File, c1999. X, 310 p.: ill. ; 29 cm. ISBN 0-8160-3903-8 (acid-free paper); ISBN 0-8160-3904-6 (pbk. :acid-free paper); ISBN 0-8160-3904-6 (pbk. :acid-free paper) LC (Library of Congress) Call Number: E185.96.K73 1998, LC (Library of Congress) Control Number: 98012355

- **Leadership** / by the editors of Time-Life Books. Alexandria, Va.: Time-Life Books, 1994. (African Americans, voices of triumph) 256 p.: ill. (some col.) ; 27 cm. ISBN 0-7835-2254-1 (trade); ISBN 0-7835-2255-X (lib. bdg.), Series: African Americans, voices of triumph. LC (Library of Congress) Call Number: E185.A2585 1994, LC (Library of Congress) Control Number: 93021147

- **Why should white guys have all the fun? : How Reginald Lewis created a billion-dollar business empire** / Reginald F. Lewis (1942 – 1993) and Blair S. Walker. New York: Wiley, c1995. Xvii, 318 p., [16] p. of plates: ill. ; 24 cm. ISBN 0-471-04227-7 (acid-free paper). LC (Library of Congress) Call Number: HC102.5.L493A3 1995, LC (Library of Congress) Control Number: 94017864

- **The Negro's adventure in general business**, by Vishnu V. Oak (1900 -), Westport, Conn., Negro Universities Press [1970, c1949] 223 p. 23 cm. LC (Library of Congress) Call Number: E185.8.O22, LC (Library of Congress) Control Number: 79100311

*Note: Reprint of v. 2 of the author's The Negro Entrepreneur (1949)

- **Great African Americans in business** / Pat Rediger (1966 -). New York, N.Y., U.S.A.: Crabtree Pub. Co., c1996. 64 p.: ill. (some col.) ; 26 cm. ISBN 0-86505-803-2; ISBN 0-86505-817-2 (pbk.), Series: Outstanding African Americans, LC (Library of Congress) Call Number: HC102.5.A2R35 1996, LC (Library of Congress) Control Number: 95024879

  *Examines the lives of more than ten African American men and women, including Oprah Winfrey, Don Cornelius, and Naomi Sims, with the obstacles they each overcame.

- **Facts and trivia: 325 questions drawn from the expertise of Harvard's Du Bois Institute** / Richard Scott Rennert (1956 -). New York: Chelsea House Publishers, c1995. 63 p.: ill. ; 21 cm. ISBN 0-7910-3211-6; ISBN 0-7910-3212-4 (pbk.), Series: African American answer book, LC (Library of Congress) Call Number: E185.A252 1995, LC (Library of Congress) Control Number: 94030203

- **RFL, Reginald F. Lewis: a tribute** / edited by Elliott Wiley. New York: Bookmark Publishing Corp., 1994. ix, 210 p.: ill. (some col.) ; 24 cm. LC (Library of Congress) Call Number: HC102.5.L493R45 1994, LC (Library of Congress) Control Number: 94184058

- **Simms' blue book and national Negro business and professional directory.** [Cleveland, Gordon Pub. Co.] 1977 – v. ill. 25 cm. LC (Library of Congress) Call Number: E185.82S592, LC (Library of Congress) Control Number: 78643543

- **All about hair care for the black woman** / Naomi Sims (1949 -); illustrated by Charles Bisaquino. Garden City, N.Y.: Doubleday, 1982. Viii, 212 p.: ill. ; 26 cm. ISBN 0-385-14819-4, LC (Library of Congress) Call Number: TT972.S53 1982, LC (Library of Congress) Control Number: 79006654

Entrepreneur and author Naomi Sims, one of the first black supermodels to achieve international recognition, went on to establish a major wig collection and cosmetic business focused on the black woman. She also authored several books on health and beauty, including this one on hair care for the black woman.

- **Profiles of great African Americans** / contributing writers, David Smallwood, Stan West, Allison Keyes. Lincolnwood, IL: Publications International, c1996. 216 p.: ill. (some col.) ; 26 cm. ISBN 0-7853-1983-2, LC (Library of Congress) Call Number: E185.96.S63 1996, LC (Library of Congress) Control Number: 96069536

- **In the Spirit: the inspirational writings** / of Susan L. Taylor. New York: Amistad, c1993. 110 p.: ill. ; 21 cm. ISBN 1-56743-032-5, LC (Library of Congress) Call Number: BL624.T395 1993, LC (Library of Congress) Control Number: 93014450

- **Free Frank: a Black pioneer on the antebellum frontier** / Juliet E. K. Walker (1940 -). Lexington, KY.: University Press of Kentucky, c1983. xii, 223 p.: ill. ; 24 cm. ISBN 0-8131-1472, LC (Library of Congress) Call Number: F460.N4F728 1983, LC (Library of Congress) Control Number: 82040181

Discusses one of the earliest pioneers of Black entrepreneurship.

Journals:

- **Black Enterprise**

    January 2001 – On the cover are Johnnie Cochran, Vanessa L. Williams, Star Jones. Article by Monique Brown and Mark Wright on the rich and famous and their investment secrets, pages 86-93.

    December 2000 – Featured on the cover is Antonio 'L.A' Reid, CEO of Arista Records, the music industry's highest ranking Black executive. Article "The New King of Pop" by Sakina Spruell on pages 94-104.

    September 2000 – On cover E. Stanley O'Neal of Merrill Lynch, BE's Corporate Executive of the Year is one of the highest paid and most powerful Blacks in corporate America. Article "Running With the Buffs" by Robin D. Clarke on pages 83-90.

    August 2000 – On cover "Fast Forward – 30 Leaders For the Future". Article "30 for the next 30" by Sonja Brown Stokely on pages 179-188 and features rising newcomers like James Winters, age 39, CEO of United Energy Inc., and Mellody Hobson, age 31, President, Ariel Capital Management.

- **Ebony**

    May 2000 – Article on Cathy Hughes entitled "Ms. Radio, most powerful woman in the industry" by Lynn Norment begins on pages 100-108.

January 2000 – "New Faces in Executive Suites" by Lynn Norment begins on page 42-48 and profiles 28 African American business leaders such as a Barry Rand, Chairman/CEO Avis Rent A Car; Franklin Raines, Chairman/CEO Fannie Mae; and Brend J. Gaines, President of Citicorp Diner Club North America, a division of Citigroup.

January 1998 – Article "Twelve Most Powerful Blacks in Corporate America" by Lynn Norment, pages 36-44 includes Lloyd G. Trotter, President/CEO General Electric's Electrical Distribution and Control; Carl Ware, President Coca-Cola Company's Africa Group; and Michele Hooper, President International Business Group of Caremark International.

- **Fortune**

    January 22, 2001 – Featured on the cover is Ken Chenault "New Man in Charge" at American Express. Article "What's in the Cards for Amex" by Nelson Schwartz on pages 58-70.

- **Inc.**

    May 2000 – On cover are brothers Vincent and Vernon Austin whose VA Construction is #25 on the "Inner City 100" list of growing companies. Snapshot profile of them done by Karen Dillon is on page 130.

- **Newsweek**

    January 8, 2001 – Featured on the cover is Oprah Winfrey, "Special Report: Women of the New Century, Oprah on Oprah" by Lynette Clemetson on pages 38-48.

Websites:

- **Printout of the Census Bureau's "Black Population in the U.S." web page.**
  http://www.census.gov/population/race/publications/

  Provides links to the Current Population Surveys, statistical briefs, the 1990 Census, race and ethnicity classifications, and related topics.

- **Printout of the Census Bureau's "Minority Links" web page.**
  http://www.census.gov/pubinfo/www/NEWafamML1.html

  Provides links to facts on the Black/African American Population on Census 2000, social and economic characteristics, new releases, and other Minority Links.

- Photocopy of Black Enterprise article "Virtual Communities", October 2000, pp. 157 – 164.
  http://www.blackenterprise.com **(Search under Archives)**

  Discusses the top African American web sites covering business, politics, culture, etc.

The following information concerning the development of Black business in the United States was prepared by: Angela Wilson and Joseph Sams, Business References Services. Science, Technology, and Business Division (Library of Congress):

Author/Title Listing:

- **Black worker.**
  Black workers: a documentary history from colonial times to the present/edited by Philip S. Foner and Ronald L. Lewis. Philadelphia: Temple University Press, 1989. Xv, 733 p.: 24 cm. LC (Library of Congress) Call Number: HD8081.A65B55 1989, LC (Library of Congress) Control Number: 88029591

  This volume is a comprehensive publication on the history of black workers from the colonial era to the present. Detailed information is provided on Black workers in history, categorized by sequential eras. A selected bibliography is provided. Access is by table of contents and index.

- **Black Capitalism; Strategy for Business in the Ghetto** by Theodore L. Cross (1924 -). New York, Atheneum, 1969. xii, 274 p. 25 cm. LC (Library of Congress) Call Number: E185.8.C9, LC (Library of Congress) Control Number: 72080268

  Discusses the philosophical basis behind Black capitalism.

- ***Du Bois, W.E.B. (William Edward Burghardt), 1868-1963, ed.***
  The Negro in business; report of a social study made under the direction of Atlanta University, together with the proceedings of the fourth Conference for the Study of the Negro Problems, held at Atlanta University,

May 30-31, 1899. New York, AMS Press [1971], 77p. 23 cm. LC (Library of Congress) Call Number: E185.8.D83 1971, LC (Library of Congress) Control Number: 70153098.

First organized effort to observe and analyze the development of Black Americans in Business.

- **Economic census: characteristics of business owners.** Washington, D.C.: U.S. Dept. of Commerce, Economics and Statistics Administration, Bureau of the Census: For sale by Supt. Of Docs., U.S. G.P.O., LC (Library of Congress) Call Number (1992 edition): HC106.8.A148 1997, LC (Library of Congress) Control Number (1992 edition): 98128230

Provides basic economic, demographic, and sociological data on the characteristics of minority, women and non-minority business owners.

- Frazier, Edward Franklin, 1894-1962.
The Negro in the United States. New York, Macmillan Co., 1949. xxxiii, 767 p. illus, maps. 22 cm. LC (Library of Congress) Call Number: E185.F833, LC (Library of Congress) Control Number: 49002984

Looks at institutional development within the Black American community.

- Gravely, Melvin J.
The Black Entrepreneur's Guide to Success / Melvin J. Gravely, II; (edited by Apryl Motley). Edgewood, Md. Duncan & Duncan, c1995. V. 214 p.: ill. ; 24 cm. LC (Library of Congress) Call Number: HD62.7.G717 1995, LC (Library of Congress) Control Number: 95067017

Outlines steps to business empowerment from self-preparation to structuring a business.

- Harmon, John Henry.
  The Negro as a Business Man. by J. H. Harmon, Jr., Arnett G. Lindsay, and Carter G. Woodson, College Park, Md., McGrath Pub. Co. [1969, c1929] v. 111 p. 24 cm. LC (Library of Congress) Call Number: E185.8.H25 1969, LC (Library of Congress) Control Number: 69017086

  Initial treatise by the Association for the Study of Negro Life and History on the assessment of the prevalent situation regarding Negro Businessmen.

- Joyce, Donald F.
  Gatekeepers of black culture: Black-owned book publishing in the United States, 1817-1981 / Donald Franklin Joyce. Westport, Conn.: Greenwood Press, 1983. xiv, 249 p. ; 22 cm. LC (Library of Congress) Call Number: Z471.J69 1983, LC (Library of Congress) Control Number: 82009227

  This is a publication on Black book publishers during the period of 1817-1981. This study focuses on the pioneer Black book publishers, the growth of Black book publishing from 1900 through 1959, developments between 1960 and 1974, and provides executive comments on the state of Black book publishing in 1981. Access is by table of contents, author index, and name and subject index. Also provided are graphs, tables, profiles of publishers and printers, and a comprehensive bibliography.

- Myrdal, Gunnar, 1898 –
  An American Dilemma: The Negro Problem and Modern Democracy / Gunnar Myrdal; with a new introduction by Sissela Bok. New Brunswick, NJ: Translation Publishers, c1996. 2 v., ill. ; 23 cm. LC (Library of Congress) Call Number: E185.6.M95 1996, LC (Library of Congress) Control Number: 95031355

Nobel prize winning work on the problems facing Black businessmen.

- Schweninger, Loren
  Black property owners in the South, 1790-1915 / Loren Schweninger. Urbana: University of Illinois Press, 1997. xvii, 426 p. : ill., maps : 23 cm. LC (Library of Congress) Call Number: E185.8S39 1997, LC (Library of Congress) Control Number: 97158808

  Traces beginnings of Black land ownership among Africans, free Negro business owners, affluent free Persons of color, and Southern Blacks.

- **Statistical record of Black America.** Detroit: Gale Research, c1990-1997. 4 v.: ill. ; 29 cm. LC (Library of Congress) Call Number: E185.5.S83, LC (Library of Congress) Control Number: 91640012

  Tables covering various subjects including business and economics to include Black-owned business characteristics.

- Swinton, David H.
  The Determinants of the Growth of Black Owned Businesses: A Preliminary Analysis / David H. Swinton, John Handy, Atlanta, Ga.: Southern Center for Studies in Public Policy, Clark College, 1984, xxiii, 129 p. ; 28 cm. LC (Library of Congress) Call Number: HD2346.U5S98 1984, LC (Library of Congress) Control Number: 84603120

  A study on the impact of physical segregation in Black business growth.

- **Try Us.** [Minneapolis, National Minority Business Campaign] v. ill. 28 cm. LC (Library of Congress) Call Number: HD2346.U5N34, LC (Library of Congress) Control Number: 79642814

    A national minority business directory.

- Washington, Booker T., 1856-1915.
    The Negro in business. New York, AMS Press [1971] 379 p. illus., ports. 18 cm. LC (Library of Congress) Call Number: HD8081.A65W37 1971, LC (Library of Congress) Control Number: 71144699

    Focuses on business as a way of life for young Black males. Contrast to DuBois' scientific analysis in his work by the same title.

- William Monroe Trotter Institute.
    Overview of Black-owned businesses in the United States in the 1990s: a report of the William Monroe Trotter Institute at the University of Massachusetts at Boston, Boston Massachusetts. Boston: The institute, [1996] 14 leaves; 29 cm. LC (Library of Congress) Call Number: HD2346.U5W549 1996, LC (Library of Congress) Control Number: 97118177

    Through tables, summarizes major characteristics of Black-owned businesses in the U.S.

*A listing of statistical compendia on African Americans compiled in conjunction with black business leaders. Prepared by Angela Wilson and Gail Austin, Business Reference Services, Science, Technology, and Business Division.

Books:

- **The African-American experience on file** / executive editor, C. Carter Smith, Jr. New York: Facts On File, 1998. 1 v (various pages): ill, maps: 30 cm. ISBN 0-8160-368-97-7 (alk. paper), LC (Library of Congress) Call Number: E185.A2533 1998, LC (Library of Congress) Catalog Record: 98029845

- **Black Americans: a statistical sourcebook** / Alfred N. Garwood, editor. Boulder, Colo.: Numbers & Concepts, c1990. xxiv. 340 p.: 20 cm. ISBN 0-929960-02-5 (trade paper), ISBN 0-929960-03-3 (library ed.), LC (Library of Congress) Call Number: E185.86B5238 1990, LC (Library of Congress) Catalog Record: 91182105

- **The Black Population in the United States.** Washington, D.C.: U.S. Dept. of Commerce, Bureau of the Census: For sale by Supt. of Docs., U.S. G.P.O., 1989- (1988<1991>: Current population reports. Series P-20, Population characteristics) (<1993-94->: Current population reports. P20, Population characteristics) v.: 28 cm. LC (Library of Congress) Call Number: HA 195.A53 subser.E185.5, LC (Library of Congress) Catalog Record: 93642496

- **Blacks on the move: a decade of demographic change:** from a report prepared by William P. O'Hare...[etc.] / abridged by Phillip Sawicki. Washington, D.C.: Joint Center for Political Studies, 1982. Xvi, 70 p.: ill.: 23 cm. ISBN 0-941410-25-0(pbk.), LC (Library of Congress) Call Number: E185.86.B545 1982, LC (Library of Congress) Catalog Record: 82214690

- Cramer, Clayton, E.
  Black demographic data, 1790-1860: a sourcebook / Clayton E. Cramer. Westport, Conn.: Greenwood Press, 1997. Viii. 165 p.: ill.: 24 cm. ISBN 0-313-30243-X (hardcover: alk. paper) LC (Library of Congress) Call Number: E185.18.C73 1997, LC (Library of Congress) Catalog Record: 96038833

- Heaton, Tim B. **Statistical handbook on racial groups in the United States** / by Tim B. Heaton, Bruce A. Chadwick, and Cardell K. Jacobson. Phoenix, AZ: Oryx Press, 2000, xix, 35 p.: 29 cm. ISBN 1-57356-266-1 (alk.paper), LC (Library of Congress) Call Number: E184.A1H417 2000, LC (Library of Congress) Catalog Record: 00028477

- **Historical statistics of Black America** / compiled & edited by Jessie Carney Smith and Carrell Peterson Horton. New York: Gale Research, c1995. 2 b. (lxxxii, 2244 p.); 29 cm. ISBN 0-8103-8542-2 (acid-free paper), ISBN 0-8103-9391-3 (v. 1 : alk. paper), ISBN - 08103-9392-1 (v. 2 : alk. paper), LC (Library of Congress) Call Number: E185.H543 1995, LC (Library of Congress) Catalog Record: 94029718

- **Life in Black America** / edited by James S. Jackson. Newbury Park, Calif.: Sage, c1991. Xi. 311p.: ill. ; 22 cm. ISBN 0-8039-3537-4, ISBN 0-8039-3538-2 (pbk.), LC (Library of Congress) Call Number: E185.86.L497 1991, LC (Library of Congress) Catalog Record: 91006934

- **The Metropolitan area fact book: a statistical portrait of blacks and whites in urban America** / edited by Katherine McFate. Washington, D.C.: Joint Center for Political Studies, 1988. X, 109 p.: maps; 23 cm. ISBN 0-941410-65-X, LC (Library of Congress)

Call Number: E185.86.M48 1988, LC (Library of Congress) Catalog Record: 88011147

- United States, Bureau of the Census.
  Sixteenth census of the United States: 1940. Population. Characteristics of the nonwhite population by race. Prepared under the supervision of Dr. Leon E. Truesdell, chief statistician for population. Washington, U.S. Govt. print off, 1943. Vi, 112 p. incl. illus. (map) tables. 29 cm. LC (Library of Congress) Call Number: E 185.6.U586, LC (Library of Congress) Catalog Record: 43050858

- United States. Bureau of the Census.
  Negro population in the United States, 1790-1915. New York, Amo Press, 1968. (The American Negro, his history and literature) 844 p. illus., maps. 27 cm. LC (Library of Congress) Call Number: HA205.A33 1968, LC (Library of Congress) Catalog Record: 68028992

- United States. Bureau of Census.
  Negroes in the United States, 1920-1932 [by] Charles E. Hall, New York, Amo Press 1969. (The American Negro, his history and literature) xvi, 845 p. illus, maps. 26 cm. LC (Library of Congress) Call Number: E185.6.U5853 1969, LC (Library of Congress) Catalog Record: 69018629

- United States, Bureau of Labor Statistics.
  Black Americans; a chartbook. {Prepared by Sylvia S. Small] Washington; For sale by the Supt. of Docs., U.S. Govt. Print Off., 1971. (Its Bulletin; 1699) x, 141 p. col. Illus. 24 cm. LC (Library of Congress) Call Number: HD8051.A62 no. 1699, LC (Library of Congress) Catalog Record: 71613945

Of course there are many resources out there to start a business. For additional resources, you should do searches online through Google (and other search engines). Also, reach out to the local business organization in your neighborhood. Here are a few more resources to check out online:

- **Black Business Association (**www.bbala.org**)**
  A Black association that offers you a membership. Through the membership you have access to bids, jobs, events, black business news, health, member spotlight, etc.

- **Black Business List (**www.blackbusinesslist.com**)**
  Advertise your Black business, or find other Black businesses by city, state, or business description.

- **The Black Business School (**https://theblackbusinessschool.com**)**
  *Select classes under the headings of: *Small Business & Entrepreneurship, *Investing, *Family & Generation Wealth at a fraction of the cost of a college degree.*

*The resources listed in this chapter are to familiarize you with our "Black Heritage". I really hope this book (including the resources) will inspire you to 'Start YOUR Own Black Business in YOUR Neighborhood'!

After reading this book, please go to Amazon.com to rate it (please...). Thank you!

Thank you again for taking the time to read this book. Please go to Amazon.com to rate this book. Also, <u>please share this book with others</u> who may be interested in starting their own Black business.

Thank you again!

Diane L. Thomas-Newbill

www.ingramcontent.com/pod-product-compliance
Lightning Source LLC
Chambersburg PA
CBHW052323220526
45472CB00001B/247